That Patchwork Place®

Jaynette Huff

Stash Magic

13 Quilts
That Make the Most
of Your Fabric
Collection

Martingale®
& COMPANY

Stash Magic:
13 Quilts That Make the Most of Your Fabric Collection
© 2009 by Jaynette Huff

That Patchwork Place® is an imprint of Martingale & Company®.

Martingale & Company
20205 144th Ave. NE
Woodinville, WA 98072-8478 USA
www.martingale-pub.com

Printed in China
14 13 12 11 10 09   8 7 6 5 4 3 2 1

**Library of Congress Cataloging-in-Publication Data
is available upon request.**

ISBN: 978-1-56477-923-6

Mission Statement

Dedicated to providing quality products and service to inspire creativity.

Credits

President & CEO: Tom Wierzbicki
Editor in Chief: Mary V. Green
Managing Editor: Tina Cook
Developmental Editor: Karen Costello Soltys
Technical Editor: Laurie Baker
Copy Editor: Sheila Chapman Ryan
Design Director: Stan Green
Production Manager: Regina Girard
Illustrator: Laurel Strand
Cover & Text Designer: Regina Girard
Photographer: Brent Kane

Dedication

To all the people involved in my husband's recent recovery from Guillain-Barré Syndrome, a serious neurological disorder. Our faith got us through, along with the many relatives, friends, and professionals who stood beside us as we dealt with his illness *and recovery!* To all the doctors, nurses, therapists, hospital staff members, friends, relatives, pastors, and so many more, a heartfelt thank-you. You are all like wonderful scraps of fabric, stitched together to form a beautiful quilt: my husband, Larry, who once again stands and walks and gives me hugs and the warmth of his presence. I am blessed!

Acknowledgments

To my publisher, Martingale & Company, and especially Mary Green, for once again allowing me to share my love of quilting with others. I am truly grateful for your professional guidance and encouragement.

A special thank-you to Laurie Baker, the technical editor for this book, for cutting, reworking, and maintaining the accuracy of my instructions. You worked wonders!

To those quilters who continue to support my quilt-related efforts: May all your scrap quilts be a pleasure to make; take joy in being able to *use up that fabric!*

And always, to Larry, my husband and friend, who supports all my endeavors with his love, patience, and an appreciation for my quilting passion. I love you.

Contents

The Quilts

Let's Talk

"Use it up" is a well-known phrase concerning conservation, the avoidance of waste, and our attempts to go green. This is an especially appropriate phrase for quilters to take to heart, with our love of accumulating fabrics and all things quilt related. Most of us have fabric stashes: some of us have fabric cascading out from our drawers and closets, or piled on our beds, or even packed away in its original shopping bags. And we hate to waste one little piece of it. This is where scrap quilts—those quilts that make use of many, many colors, prints, sizes, and mixes of the fabrics we already have on hand—hold their own.

Just what is a fabric scrap? According to most quilters, it's a small detached piece, a fragment of something that is left over, the least little bit. But no matter how small, we still can't throw it out! So back to those three words above: use it up!

At first glance, those words may seem like a very simple goal: to make use of those small, detached pieces of fabric. But for the serious quilter (and one with a significant fabric stash), the goal is more than just using up the scraps. The ultimate goal becomes one of arranging those fabric pieces into carefully planned, selected, and executed quilt designs—of combining an interesting mix of many, many fabric scraps in a multitude of colors into a beautiful quilt. My hope is that you will view the quilts in this book as successful renditions of that ultimate goal.

For me, creating a beautiful scrap quilt does not mean simply grabbing any piece of fabric and sewing it to the next piece of fabric, regardless of whether I think it blends well or not. I enjoy the process of trusting my personal judgment and making good choices. I like being able to audition my fabric scraps, to say "yes, this one works," or "no, not this time." Making fabric choices doesn't need to be tiresome or labor intensive. Rather, it involves doing a bit of preplanning, early decision making, and consideration of several questions, including:

- For whom is this quilt being made?
- Where will this quilt be used or displayed?
- What size is required?
- What types and amounts of fabric scraps do I have?
- What quiltmaking techniques do I wish to use?

Once you've answered these questions, you're ready to proceed. You merely need to determine which particular quilt design fits the bill. Let me help. In this book you'll find 13 different opportunities to use your fabric scraps and achieve the ultimate goal. Such variety is achieved in several ways:

1. *Variety in construction techniques.* Not all quilters enjoy the same methods of construction, nor do they feel as confident with some techniques as others. The construction methods used in making these quilts include paper foundation piecing, rotary cutting, and template piecing. In addition, specialized techniques are introduced to add dimension and beauty, including English paper piecing, bias tubes for appliqué, and three-dimensional prairie points.

2. *Variety in block design and block alteration.* This book is built around seven larger quilt projects, and with the exception of "Flying in Formation" (page 56), each is accompanied by a smaller project. In each of the smaller projects, some aspect of the original block of the larger quilt is altered or modified (larger to smaller, elimination of some part of the block, change in fabric placement, complexity of design, etc.).

3. *Variety in overall quilt size.* The quilts vary in size from small wall hangings to larger lap quilts and coverlets to even larger bed-sized quilts.

4. *Variety in block setting and borders.* Some designs are simple straight sets with one-block designs arranged next to one another, while others offer more complex settings with sashing, corner squares, and multiple borders. There are also several two-block quilts where, by alternating the placement of the blocks, beautiful secondary designs emerge. Border designs also vary from simple fabric strips, to appliqué, to multiple pieced borders.

5. *Variety in fabric organization and selection.* The quilter is encouraged to organize and/or classify many of her fabrics into particular groupings, such as color groups (greens, yellows, reds, blues), fabric types (batiks, border prints, homespuns), or historical time frames (1930s, Civil War era). The attempt is to create more pleasing scrap quilts that emphasize their design and appearance, as well as their economy.

In summary, this book addresses those "strips and bits" of our fabrics and illustrates how to turn them into wonderful quilts of many colors and sizes. The goal is not just to use it up, but rather to arrange those fabric strips and bits into planned and selected scrap-quilt designs and patterns that are beautiful to use and enjoy!

Fabric Selection and Preparation

Be scrap happy! Mix it up. Let your blocks reflect past quilting endeavors. Clean out your scrap bags. Collect fabric leftovers from your relatives' and friends' quilting projects. Purchase those wonderful packets of charm squares and bundles of new fabric collections. Just gather . . . gather . . . gather.

When you are ready to begin a new quilting project, keep a few basic guidelines in mind:

- Use only top-quality, 100%-cotton fabrics.
- Prewash your fabrics. Avoid the heartbreak of unexpected shrinking and running dye that might occur later.

- Provide contrast in value (darks, mediums, and lights), scale (large, medium, and small), and intensity (high voltage vs. calm and serene). All three types of contrast can add interest, variety, and life to your work.
- Look for variety in your fabric choices: tone-on-tone prints, tiny allover prints, large-scale prints, busy stripes, and so on. Anything goes!
- Organize your scraps into categories, allowing for a more pleasing, structured, thought-out look: for example, 1930s or Civil War–era reproductions, batiks, homespuns, or different color groups (brights, soft pastels, greens, reds, and so on).
- Choose your quilt project—and begin.

Piecing and Appliqué Methods

It's nice having several different piecing methods in one's quilting repertoire. Some methods are easier, faster, more accurate, or more portable than others. This section of the book provides clear instructions for the piecing and appliqué methods recommended for each quilt project.

Paper Foundation Piecing

When accuracy and precision are called for in quilt-block construction, paper foundation piecing provides the means to success. It is a simple alphabetic and numeric process of following the sewing order, one sewn piece after another. Take a few moments to read over the instructions and perhaps even sew one of the smaller blocks as a "test piece" to make sure you understand each step in the process.

Step 1: Trace the Pattern onto the Foundation

A pattern is provided for each paper-foundation-pieced block design. Each part of the block is labeled with the sewing order and fabric designations. You have several options for paper foundations, but I recommend ordinary freezer paper due to its adhering qualities. After you iron fabrics to freezer paper, they remain secure. Freezer paper comes on a roll and you can tear off any length needed. Trace the pattern onto the dull side of freezer paper. Be sure to include the alphabetic and numeric designations, which indicate the sewing order, as well as the letters, which indicate the fabric.

Notice that the pattern is actually the mirror image of the finished block. Everything appears in reverse order. This is because you sew on the marked side of the paper with the fabric placed on the reverse side. When you turn your work over, you will see that everything is correct.

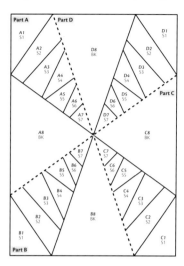

Foundation pattern

When a reversed pattern is called for, simply trace the pattern onto a piece of tracing paper first, using a pen or marker that will allow you to see the marks from the other side of the paper. Flip the paper over and trace the design through to the blank side. Trace this pattern onto freezer paper or your foundation material.

Step 2: Add Reference Marks to the Foundation

Adding hash marks, or reference marks, to your foundation is extremely important. Don't skip this step. On each pattern, individual pieces and parts are separated by solid or dashed lines. Solid lines separate pattern pieces within parts. *Do not* cut along these lines; these are your sewing lines. Short dashed lines separate parts of the pattern within particular blocks. Later you will be cutting and separating the parts along the dashed lines.

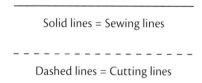

Solid lines = Sewing lines

Dashed lines = Cutting lines

Every dashed line should have reference marks added across it. These marks will later serve as the precise matching points between parts when joining them together. Make use of many different types of reference marks: single slash, double slash, triple slash, single X, double X, etc. Use a different color of fine-line marker for each type of hash mark.

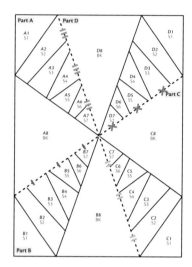

Step 3: Refer to the Sewing Order and Fabric Key

Every pattern comes with a fabric key indicating the fabrics used for each piece. Blocks with more than one part also come with a sewing order so you will know the order in which to join the parts.

**Elongated Pinwheel Block
Foundation Pattern**

Fabric Key

BK—Background
S1–S7—Scraps of assorted fabrics

Sewing Order

Piece each part in
numerical order.
Join A to B (AB).
Join C to D (CD).
Join AB to CD (ABCD).

Step 4: Cut Out the First Part

In paper foundation piecing you'll be working both alpha-betically and numerically. If your block has more than one part, find part A. With scissors, carefully cut out the shape exactly on the line. Remember, cut only on dashed lines, not on solid lines. Set the rest of the foundation aside.

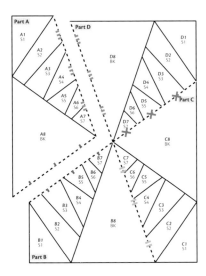

Step 5: Iron the First Piece

Locate the first piece, A1, and its corresponding fabric. From your fabric, roughly cut out a piece large enough to cover that area completely with at least a ¼" seam allow-ance all around. With the wrong side of the fabric against the shiny side of the freezer paper, iron the first piece in place under the area marked A1. This is the only piece that is ironed in place first.

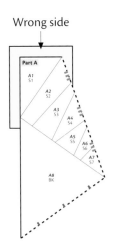

Wrong side

Step 6: Begin Sewing

Look at your foundation to determine which fabric is designated for the second piece, A2. Unless the instruc-tions specify a precut piece to use, cut a piece of this fabric large enough to cover that area. Do not try to cut fabrics the exact size of the piece like you would with a template. Instead, cut large enough pieces to ensure coverage with extra for the seam allowances. You will be trimming away the excess and can often use the leftovers in another place.

Hold the foundation so the paper side is facing you and the attached fabric piece 1 is behind it. Rotate the paper so that pattern piece A1 is below pattern piece A2. Locate your sewing line—the solid straight line running between A1 and A2. With right sides together, place fabric piece 2 under piece 1 with at least ¼" extending beyond the sewing line. With the foundation paper side facing you, hold the whole unit up to the light and see if you must reposition your fabric. At this point, most of piece 2 will be behind piece 1.

Note: The previously sewn work will always be below the line on which you are sewing.

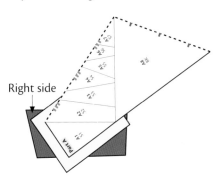

Right side

Again, make sure that the fabric piece you're adding will be large enough to cover the area it's designed to cover plus extra for seam allowance. Too big is better than too small. If you are unsure whether your new piece is large enough, test it first. Simply pin the new fabric along the sewing line and flip the fabric up. You can now see whether it is large enough.

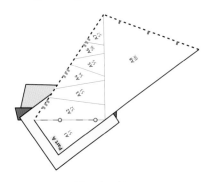

Pin-checking

9

With the foundation paper side up, sew along the solid line, using 15 to 20 stitches per inch. The small stitches will make the removal of the paper foundation easier. When the sewing line begins or ends at the outer edge of the pattern part, begin stitching in the seam allowance area and continue stitching beyond the pattern edge into the fabric. When the stitching line intersects another sewing line within the pattern part, stop at the line; backstitch if desired.

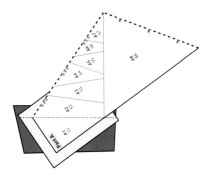

Step 7: Trim the Seam Allowance

Remove the unit from the sewing machine and lay it flat on the table with the foundation side up. With your fingers holding down the previously sewn fabrics, which are still right sides together, carefully fold back the foundation at the sewing line. With your thumbnail, crease the foundation paper along the sewing line. Don't flip up the new fabric yet. Pick up the unit and trim the fabric layers to a scant ¼" seam allowance. Use a small pair of scissors and simply eyeball the ¼".

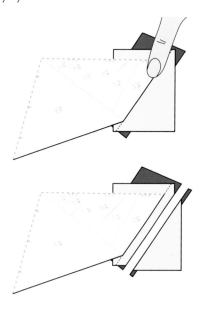

Step 8: Flip and Press

Once you've trimmed the fabrics, fold the foundation paper back down. Flip up the newly attached fabric piece and press it into place, ensuring a sharp, creased fold along the seam line. Press from the paper side first, gently pulling on the new fabric piece as you glide the iron toward your hand and over the paper. Then turn the whole unit over, check that there are no excess fabric folds or pleats on the seam line, and press from the fabric side.

Check to make sure the entire pattern piece is covered with plenty of extra fabric around the sewing lines. This excess is your seam allowance. If you have a lot of excess fabric, carefully trim it away, making sure you leave plenty around the edges of the piece.

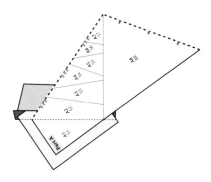

Step 9: Repeat the Process

Continue in the same manner until the entire part is completed. With each new fabric piece, refer to step 6 as needed. Remember to sew the pieces in numeric order or they won't fit together correctly.

Step 10: Trim the Finished Part

Once an entire part has been sewn, trim an exact ¼" seam allowance around all of the sides. Accuracy is important here, so use your rotary cutter, mat, and ruler.

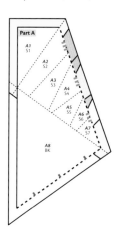

Step 11: Sew the Parts Together

Once several parts are complete, it's time to sew them together. You will need to be as accurate and precise as possible. This is where those reference marks that you drew in step 2 really pay off. First, carefully align the appropriate parts with the corresponding hash marks (single red slashes with single red slashes, double blue lines with double blue lines, etc.). Hold the parts with right sides together.

Next, pinpoint match the reference marks. Insert a sewing pin through the hash mark on one part, exactly on the edge of the foundation paper, and then through the fabrics and into the paper of the other part. Ideally, the pin will pierce the corresponding mark on the other paper. If it doesn't, simply reposition the pin and fabric until it does. Remember, these are bias edges, so they will ease right in. Add as many pins along an edge as you need for exact placement.

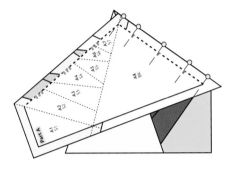

Sew along the pinned edge of the paper. Start at an outside edge and sew to the end of the other outside edge. The needle should just barely brush the paper's edge. Sew carefully, slowly, and accurately. Don't remove the pins until the last moment, or you will lose your perfect match as the pieces shift or slide away from each other.

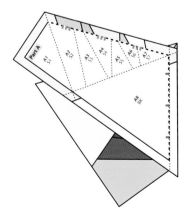

Remove the unit from the sewing machine and check to make sure the points match precisely.

Step 12: Press the Seam Allowances

Once the parts are sewn together, press the seam allowances. I generally let them go where they want to go, pressing toward the direction of least resistance. Continue in this manner until all parts are completely joined together, checking the sewing order for guidance.

Step 13: Square Up the Block

Using your rotary cutter, mat, and ruler, carefully trim ¼" from the block's outer solid line.

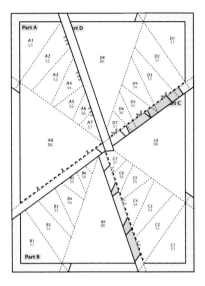

Step 14: Remove the Paper

Do not remove the foundation paper from the outside edges of any part until it has been joined to other parts or until the outer edges have been joined to sashing or borders. Remember, these fabrics have been cut and placed with no real concern for grain line, so the edges are primarily bias and can easily stretch or become distorted.

Once other sections stabilize the part, you can gently remove the foundation paper. Usually the smaller stitch length allows for easy removal with your fingers, but for tightly adhered pieces, use a stiletto or tweezers. Avoid tugging or tearing too hard on the seam lines and stitches.

English-Paper-Pieced Hexagon Units

Having a take-along project for those times when you don't have access to your sewing machine, or for when you simply want to do handwork, is a good thing. English paper piecing offers such an opportunity. The step-by-step technique is the same for all the projects that use hexagonal units; only the number and arrangement of the fabric-covered patches changes.

You can make the templates needed for these projects or you can purchase them. I strongly recommend using commercial precut templates because they are die cut and therefore more accurate (see "Resource" on page 96). If you want to make your own, use the pattern below to cut the templates from heavyweight paper. Accuracy at this stage is very important. You will need one ½" (measured on one side) template for each piece.

½" hexagon pattern

1. Place a template on the desired fabric and freehand cut around it, adding an approximate ¼" seam allowance on each of the six sides. Repeat for each piece needed, layering fabrics so several pieces can be cut at once, if desired.

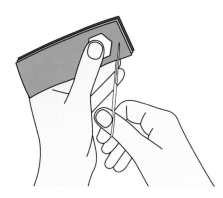

2. Baste the fabric to the templates. Thread your needle and knot one end. Center a paper template on the wrong side of a fabric patch. Carefully fold the fabric seam allowance over one edge and finger-press it in place. Hold the template in place, making sure the fabric fold is precisely at the edge of the paper template. Baste the folded-over seam allowance in place using a running stitch. Begin by inserting the needle

from the front side of the patch to the back, stitching through all three layers (fabric, paper template, seam allowance).

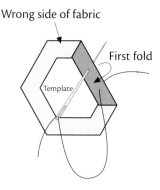

Wrong side of fabric

First fold

Template

Turn the fabric and template so the next edge is in position to be basted. Fold over the seam allowances at the next edge, creating a crisp, precise corner. Come up through the folded corner of the fabric, where the two edges meet, to baste more securely. Baste this side just as you did the first one.

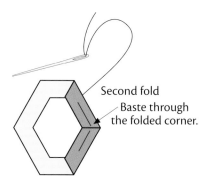

Second fold

Baste through the folded corner.

Continue basting around all six sides. On the last fold, take an extra basting stitch or two. Bring out the needle through the front of the patch and trim the thread, leaving a ½" tail. Repeat with the remaining templates and fabric patches.

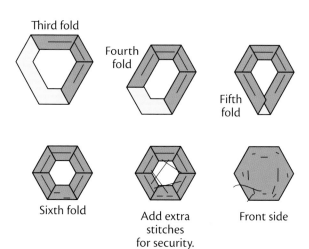

Third fold

Fourth fold

Fifth fold

Sixth fold

Add extra stitches for security.

Front side

3. Join the fabric patches. Thread a hand-sewing needle with thread in a color that matches your fabrics; knot one end. Choose a center hexagon and an adjacent hexagon. With wrong sides facing you, hold the hexagon edges to be joined *side by side,* carefully aligning the edges and corners. Note that the hexagons are held *flat,* not with right sides together as in traditional English paper piecing.

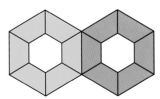

Insert the needle under one folded seam allowance and bring it out through the corner of the fabric. Insert it into the corresponding corner of the other fabric-covered hexagon. Pull the thread until the two corners are aligned.

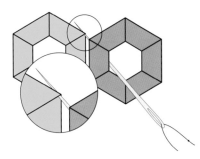

From the back side of the patches, use a flat, straight stitch to sew back and forth across the two edges. Be sure to catch only the edges of the seam allowances, not the paper template.

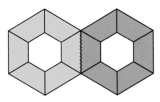

When you reach the end of the side, take an extra stitch or two and knot the thread. If you are adding another adjacent hexagon, match up corresponding edges and corners and join each side of that hexagon as you did the first one. Once you've finished adding hexagons, knot the thread end and bury a length of

thread by traveling under the seam allowance a distance before trimming.

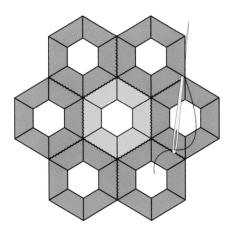

4. Prepare the background fabric. Fold the piece in half lengthwise and crosswise to mark the center. Follow the placement guide to arrange the block pieces on the background. Embroider, fuse, or appliqué any other elements that create the design or that will be tucked under the hexagon unit (stems, leaves, and so on).

5. Appliqué the hexagon unit(s) to the background. Baste the units in place with a contrasting thread color first, and then use your desired hand- or machine-appliqué method to stitch each unit in place with thread that matches the fabrics, being careful not to stitch through the paper templates.

6. Remove the basting stitches from the front of each hexagon. Turn the background fabric over, locate the hexagons, and using the smallest scissors you have, such as appliqué or embroidery scissors, carefully slit the background fabric behind them. Insert the point of your scissors and cut away the background fabric at

least ¼" *inside* the appliqué stitching line. Make sure you don't cut the hexagon fabric.

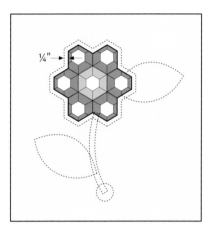

Remove the paper template by using your fingernail to pop out each template. Make sure all of the paper templates have been removed before quilting; by that point, it's too late.

Appliquéd Circles

Traditional appliqué designs frequently use circles to represent berries, flower centers, and dots. They are also great for covering up the ends of appliquéd bias-tube stems, vines, and wrought-iron designs.

1. Trace circle pattern A (at right) onto template plastic and cut it out. Using the template, trace the required number of circles onto the *wrong* side of your fabric. Cut out each fabric circle on the line drawn.

2. Using fairly small stitches, baste a running stitch ⅛" from the edge of each circle. Leave a 2" to 3" thread tail at the beginning and end of your basting line.

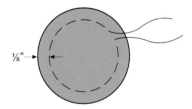

3. Use circle pattern B (at right) to make several circles from lightweight cardboard or heat-resistant template material. This smaller circle represents the finished size of your fabric circle so it needs to be accurate. Use an emery board to gently sand and smooth the edges of your circles to eliminate any sharp angles.

4. With the wrong side of the fabric circle facing up, place a cardboard circle in the center of the fabric circle. Spray some spray starch into the lid of the spray starch can. Use a small, clean paintbrush to brush the seam allowance with the liquid. Then gently pull on the ends of the basting threads, gathering up the seam allowance around the cardboard circles.

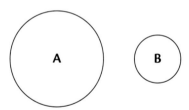

Cardboard circle

5. With the gathered seam allowance facing up, hold the thread tails to keep the circle tight, and then press each circle. Hold the iron over each circle for several seconds, letting the heat dry the starch and secure the small circle shape. Let dry.

6. Gently loosen the basting thread just a bit and slip out the template.

7. Pull the threads, gently reshaping the circle if needed, and turn over the circle with the front side up. Press.

8. When you are ready to appliqué the circles in place, trim off the excess thread tails, position each circle, and appliqué with matching thread.

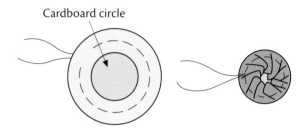

A   B

Bias-Strip Tubing

When making vines, stems, and wrought-iron designs, I strongly recommend using bias press bars for precise and even results. If you want to make your tubes without the use of bars, simply fold bias strips into thirds to achieve the correct width, spray with spray starch, and press.

1. Align the 45°-angle line of your ruler with the edge of a single layer of the desired fabric. Cut along the edge of the ruler. Measuring from the cut edge, cut as many strips as needed for the project in the width indicated.

For ¼"-wide finished bias tubes, cut fabric strips ⅞" wide. For ⅛"-wide finished bias tubes, cut fabric strips ⅝" wide.

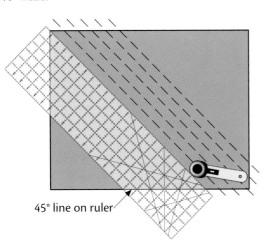

45° line on ruler

2. If tubes longer than the individual lengths that you cut are needed, sew strips together end to end, offsetting the strips by ¼" as shown. Press the seam allowances open.

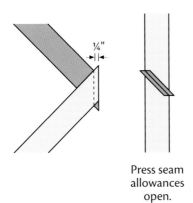

¼"

Press seam allowances open.

3. Fold the bias strips in half lengthwise, *wrong sides together*. Sew along the raw edges, using a very short stitch length (18 to 20 stitches per inch). For ¼"-wide finished tubes, stitch a generous ¼" from the *folded* edge. For ⅛"-wide finished tubes, stitch a generous ⅛" from the *folded* edge.

Check the Fit

Stitch a few inches; then check the tube width by inserting your bias bar into the tube. It should be a snug fit, but not tight. If everything is ok, remove the bar and continue stitching along the length of the folded fabric strip.

4. Insert the bias bar into the sewn tube, roll the seam to the center of the flat side of the bar, and steam press the seam allowance to one side. As you press, slide the bar along the length of the tube.

Bias bar

5. Remove the bar and steam press the fabric tube from the front side.

6. Trim off any excess seam allowance that might peek out from under the fabric tube when it's appliquéd in place.

7. Once constructed, store lengths of bias tubing around a cardboard tube, such as an empty paper-towel roll. Gently wind the lengths around the cardboard tube and secure with a pin until ready to use.

8. When using, cut the fabric tube slightly longer than the required length. Position the tube on your pieced block or border and use your steam iron to set gentle curves as needed. Thread baste the tubes in place, leaving ends flat and unfinished. They will be covered by other pieces later. Once basted in place, appliqué along each edge.

Borders

Borders in this book have either butted corners or mitered corners. Instructions are included here for both types.

Borders with Butted Corners

The steps given here are for adding the side borders first, and then the top and bottom borders. When the project instructs you to add the top and bottom borders first, and then the side borders, measure the width first, join the top and bottom borders to the quilt top, and then measure the length, including the top and bottom borders just added.

1. Cut the border strips as indicated in the project cutting instructions.

2. Measure the length of the quilt top through the center. Cut border strips to that measurement, piecing as necessary. Fold the quilt top and the borders in half to determine the midpoints; crease or pin-mark centers. Pin the border strips to the sides of the quilt top, matching the center marks and ends and easing as

necessary. Sew the border strips in place. Press the seam allowances in the direction indicated.

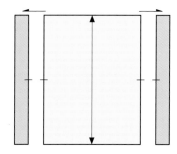

Measure center of
quilt, top to bottom.
Mark centers.

3. Measure the width of the quilt top through the center, including the side borders just added. Cut border strips to that measurement, piecing as necessary. Refer to step 2 to find the centers and sew the border strips in place. Press the seam allowances in the direction indicated.

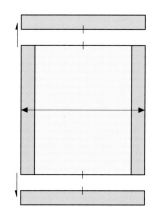

Measure center of quilt, side to
side, including border strips.
Mark centers.

Borders with Mitered Corners

1. Cut the border strips as indicated in the project instructions.

2. On the quilt, mark the center of each side of the quilt top. Mark the ¼" seam intersections on the four quilt corners.

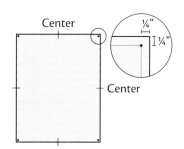

3. Mark the center of each border strip and ¼" in from where the corners of the quilt will be.

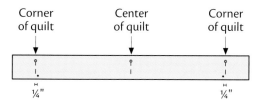

4. With right sides together, pin the side border strips to the quilt sides, matching center and corner marks. Stitch the border to the quilt, sewing from corner mark to corner mark. Press the seam allowances in the direction indicated in the project instructions. Repeat for the top and bottom borders, making sure the stitching lines meet exactly at the corners.

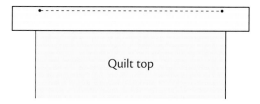

5. With right sides together, fold the quilt diagonally so that the border strips are aligned. Using a ruler with a 45° angle, draw a line on the wrong side of the border strip from the corner mark to the outside edge as shown.

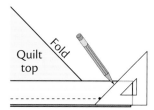

6. Pin the borders together and stitch on the drawn line. Open out the top and make sure the seam is flat and accurate before trimming the seam allowances. Press the seam allowances open. Repeat for the remaining corners.

Happy Endings

The blocks are sewn, the sashing and borders are attached, and all the foundation papers have been removed. The end of the project is now within sight. Oh, happy day! The finishing touches are all that remain. Take the time to do them right. Give them the attention they deserve, and make them truly your "happy endings."

Basting

The time has come when the three layers—quilt top, batting, and backing—need to be temporarily bound together by basting. Good basting sets the stage for trouble-free quilting.

1. Prewash the backing fabric and batting, if needed or desired.

2. Cut the backing fabric and batting 4" to 6" larger than the pieced top. This allows for some drawing up of the top as you quilt or for some shifting and movement of the top.

3. Place the backing fabric right side down on a flat work surface. Secure it with masking tape in several places along the edges. Then place the batting on top of the secured backing. Smooth it out from the center. It, too, can be secured with masking tape. Finally, center the pieced top, right side up, onto the batting and backing. Smooth it out.

4. Baste the layers together, using thread if you plan to hand quilt, or size 0 or 1 rustproof safety pins for machine quilting. Space the basting stitches or pins about 2" to 3" apart.

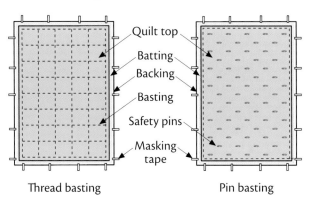

Thread basting   Pin basting

Quilting

Quilting has a twofold purpose: to permanently bond the layers and also to enhance the piecework, bringing dimension and depth to the quilt top. Paper-foundation-pieced projects and scrappy quilts often have many, many seam allowances, which can cause hand-quilting difficulties. I recommend machine quilting for the projects in this book, although hand quilting could be managed in large open areas.

Rod Pocket

There are many ways to hang your quilts. Attaching a sleeve or pocket of some type enables you to insert a rod or dowel at the back of the quilt top. By using a rod pocket, the rod or dowel won't touch, stain, or otherwise damage the back of your quilt. Follow the steps below to make a rod pocket.

1. Measure the width of your quilt at the top and subtract 2". Cut a fabric strip to that length and 5" to 9" wide, depending upon the size of the rod you plan to use for hanging.

2. Press under each end ¼". Press under ¼" again and stitch ⅛" from the first folded edge.

3. Fold the strip in half lengthwise, wrong sides together. Pin it together at the ends and at several points in between. Press.

4. Center the rod pocket on the back of the quilt at the upper edge, aligning raw edges; pin in place. As you add the binding to the upper edge of the quilt, you will automatically attach the rod pocket.

5. After you apply the binding, hand hem stitch the bottom edge of the rod pocket to the quilt back. Be sure to catch only the backing and batting and leave the ends of the sleeve open, sewing only the bottom layer of the rod pocket to the quilt.

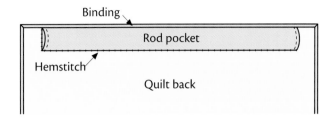

Binding

After the quilt is quilted, it's time to bind the outer edges. This method allows your binding to be very neat and full of batting.

1. Square up the quilt layers by trimming the excess batting and backing even with the quilt top.

2. Using your rotary-cutting equipment, cut enough 2"-wide strips to go around the quilt, with enough extra for corner turns and final joining. Join the strips with diagonal seams into one long continuous binding strip. Press the seam allowances open.

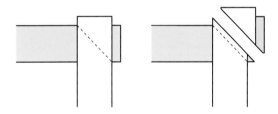

3. Press the binding in half lengthwise, wrong sides and raw edges together.

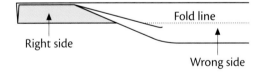

4. Beginning on one side, place the binding on the quilt top, aligning the binding raw edges with the quilt raw edge. Using a ¼" seam allowance and leaving the first 8" unstitched, stitch the binding to the quilt top, backstitching at the beginning and stopping ¼" from the corner; backstitch and remove the quilt from the machine.

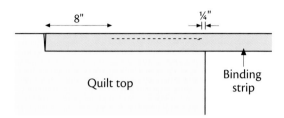

5. With the corner directly in front of you, fold the binding straight up, creating a 45° angle. Then fold the binding straight down, with the fold even with the edges of the quilt. The raw edges of the binding are now even with the next side.

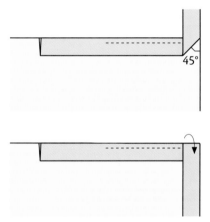

6. Begin stitching just off the fabric at the corner. The new seam is now perpendicular to the previous stitched line. Continue until you are ¼" from the next corner and repeat step 5. Repeat for all four corners of the quilt, stopping 5" to 10" from where you originally began stitching. Backstitch.

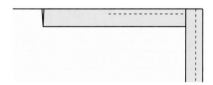

7. Remove the quilt from the machine and leave an 8"-long tail of binding extending beyond the beginning tail. Lay the quilt flat on the ironing board and carefully fold the two tails together at the center. Press, creating an easily seen crease line.

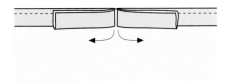

8. Unfold the strip ends. Lay one flat, with the right side up. Lay the other, right side down, over it, matching the crease points on the edges. Carefully draw a diagonal line through the point where the fold lines meet. Stitch through the marked line.

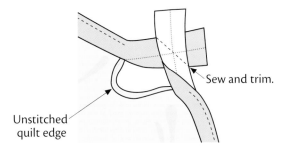

Unstitched quilt edge

Sew and trim.

9. Check to make sure the newly attached binding is the correct length and closes the gap. If so, trim off the tails ¼" from the seam. Finger-press the seam allowance open. Refold the binding and finish sewing the binding between the beginning and ending points.

10. Gently bring the binding from the front of the quilt to the back and pin it in place. The binding should easily fold over the seam allowance and just cover the stitching line. Using a thread color that matches the binding, whipstitch the folded edge of the binding to the back of the quilt, being careful that your stitches do not go through to the front of the quilt. As you reach the corners, gently pull the binding straight out. With your thumbnail in the corner, fold over the unstitched binding edge, creating a mitered corner. Secure it with stitching. Do this for all the corners of the quilt.

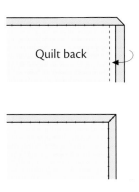

Quilt back

Labeling

Labeling your quilt is an important finishing touch because it defines your quilts historically. Who will know in the future who made this quilt and the details about it if you do not sign it? Let your label tell the quilt's story, such as the date it was completed, by whom, for whom, techniques used, special fabric choices, and so on.

Attic Window Batiks

Nothing is more beautiful than a stained-glass window, and this quilt is no exception. Using your scraps of bold and bright batiks and solids, create your own glorious window. Team up those colors with more subdued window sashings of brown wood-grain prints and an inky black, add an authentic-looking brick border fabric, and suddenly you have a window with a truly priceless view of a beautiful world.

Materials

Yardages are based on 42"-wide fabrics.

3⅛ yards *total* or ⅛ yard *each* of at least 25 assorted bright-colored batiks or solid-colored fabrics for window glass

2⅜ yards of black fabric for sashing, inner border, outer border, and binding*

2⅓ yards of brick print for middle border

¾ yard of wood-grain print 1 for vertical window sash*

⅝ yard of wood-grain print 2 for horizontal window sash*

4⅝ yards of fabric for backing

63" x 83" piece of batting

Paper-piecing foundation material

*Make sure there is good contrast between these three fabrics.

Cutting

Patterns for templates A and B are on page 24.

From wood-grain print 1, cut:
9 strips, 2½" x 42". From these strips, cut 25 template A pieces.

From wood-grain print 2, cut:
7 strips, 2½" x 42". From these strips, cut 25 template B pieces.

From the *lengthwise grain* of the black fabric, cut:
12 strips, 1¼" x 78"; crosscut into:
    2 strips, 1¼" x 66"
    6 strips, 1¼" x 45"
    20 strips, 1¼" x 12½"
4 strips, 2½" x 78"
4 binding strips, 2" x 78"

From the *lengthwise grain* of the brick print, cut:
4 strips, 4½" x 75"

Making the Attic Window Blocks

1. Refer to "Paper Foundation Piecing" (page 7) to trace 25 copies of the stained-glass pattern (page 23) onto your paper-piecing foundation material. Construct the stained-glass units, following the given sewing order and using a variety of batik and/or solid fabrics in each rectangle.

2. Stack the units on top of each other so that part A is on the left-hand side. Sew a template A piece to the right-hand side of 13 of these units, stitching from the top of the unit to the dot. Rotate the remaining 12 rectangles 180° so that part A is on the right-hand side and add the template A pieces in the same manner. Press the seam allowances toward the A pieces. Sew the template B pieces to the bottom of each unit, stitching from the left-hand side of the unit to the dot. Press the seam allowances toward the B pieces.

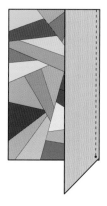
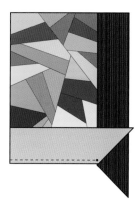

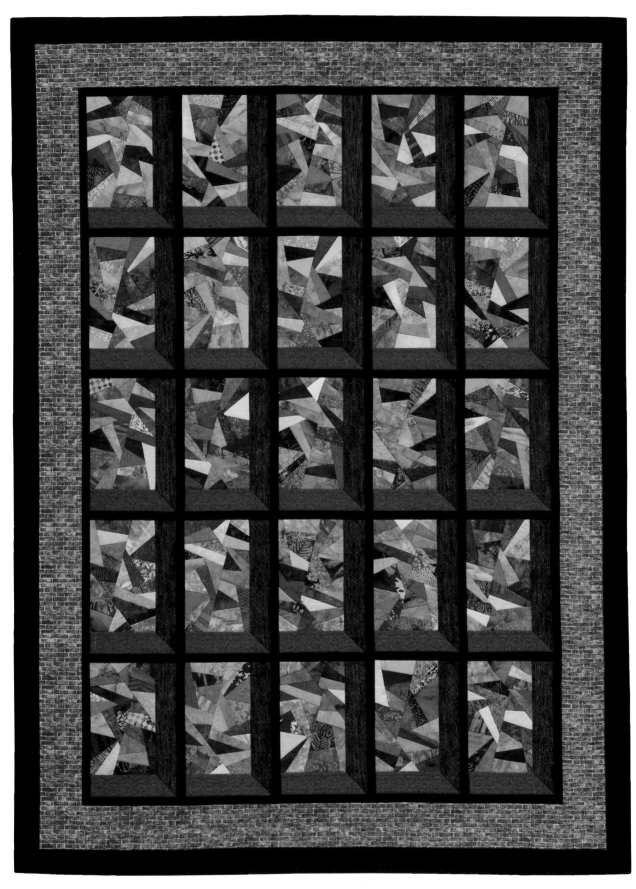

Quilt finished size: 56½" x 76½"

Block: Attic Window • **Block finished size:** 8" x 12"

3. With right sides together and angled ends and dots aligned, stitch the template A and B pieces together, stitching from the dot to the outer edges of the pieces.

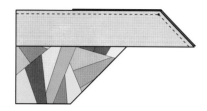

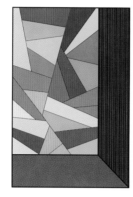

Block A.
Make 13.

Block B.
Make 12.

Assembling the Quilt Top

1. Join the blocks and black 1¼" x 12½" sashing strips as shown to make the block rows. Press the seam allowances toward the sashing strips.

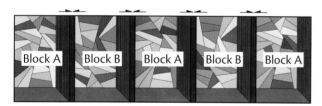

Make 3.

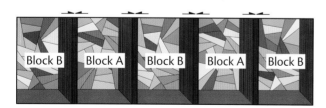

Make 2.

2. Measure the width of the block rows through the center and trim the black 1¼" x 45" sashing strips to that measurement. Refer to the assembly diagram to alternately stitch the sashing strips and block rows together. Press the seam allowances toward the sashing strips. Measure the length of the quilt top through the center and trim the black 1¼" x 66" inner-border strips to that measurement. Sew these strips to the sides of the quilt top. Press the seam allowances toward the border strips.

3. Refer to "Borders with Butted Corners" (page 15) to add the brick print middle borders to the quilt top, adding the top and bottom borders first and then the side borders. Repeat to add the black 2½"-wide outer border strips to the quilt top.

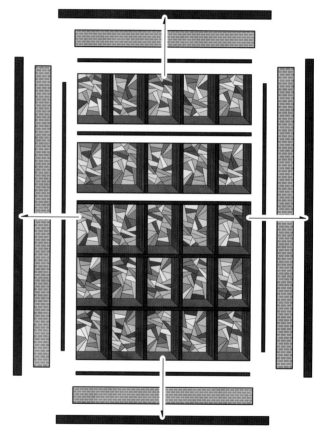

Quilt assembly

Finishing the Quilt

Refer to "Happy Endings" (page 17) as needed.

1. Layer the quilt top with batting and backing; baste.

2. Quilt as desired.

3. Square up the quilt top.

4. Add a rod pocket if desired and bind the quilt with the black 2"-wide binding strips.

5. Stitch a label to the quilt back.

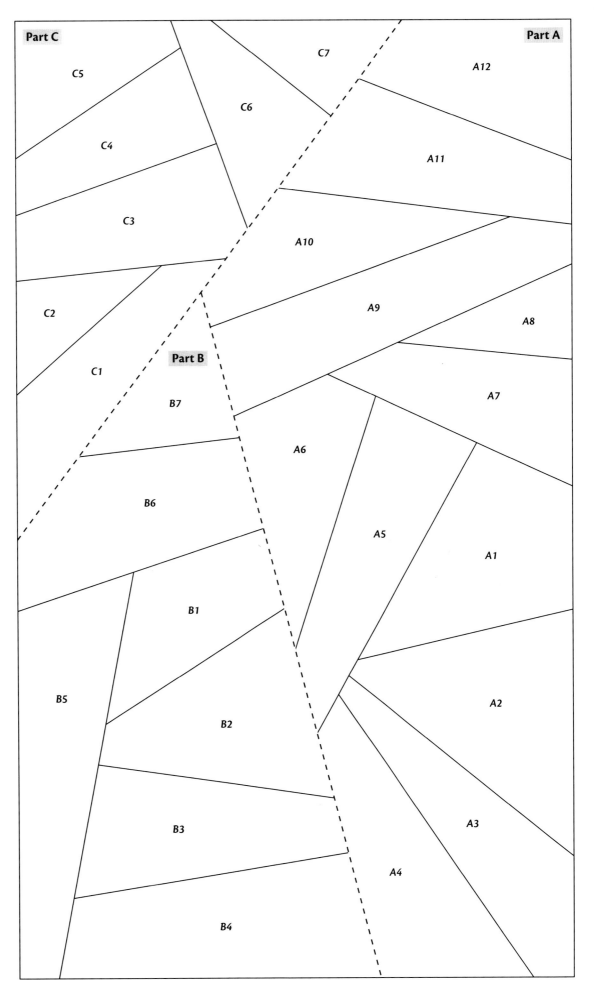

Part C

Part A

C5

C7

A12

C4

C6

A11

C3

A10

C2

A9

A8

C1

A7

Part B

B7

A6

B6

A5

A1

B1

A2

B5

B2

A3

B3

A4

B4

**Stained Glass Block
Foundation Pattern**

Sewing Order

Piece each part in
numerical order.
Join A to B (AB).
Join AB to C (ABC).

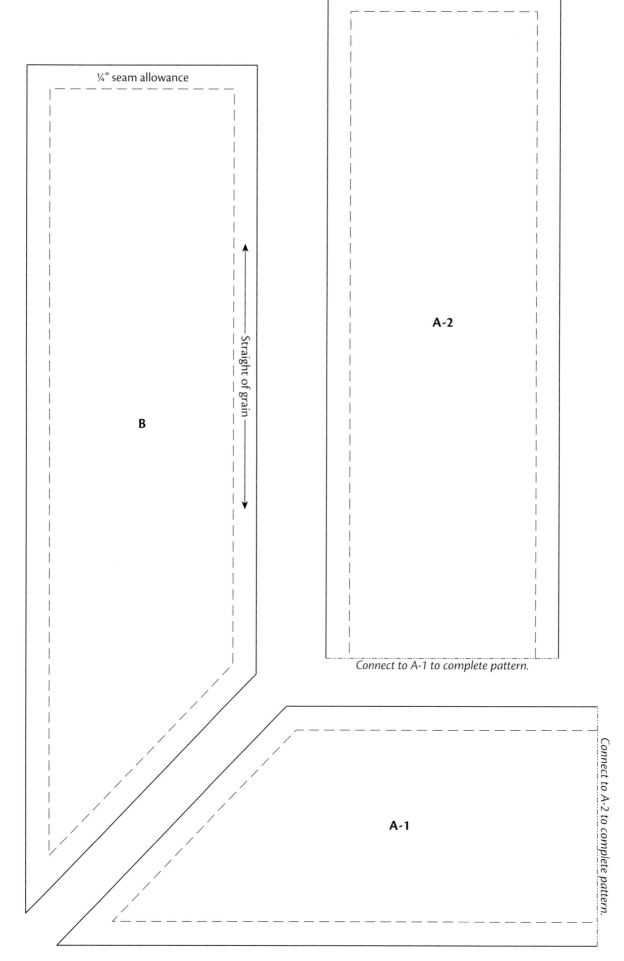

¼" seam allowance

Straight of grain

B

A-2

Connect to A-1 to complete pattern.

A-1

Connect to A-2 to complete pattern.

Wrought-Iron Window

Wrought-iron "lacework" adds old-world beauty and charm to fences, gates, balconies—and this quilt. Using bias tubing and foundation-pieced Stained Glass blocks created from soft pastel scraps, you, too, can create your own wrought-iron window.

Materials

Yardages are based on 42"-wide fabrics.

1 fat quarter (18" x 22") *each* of at least 9 assorted pastel-colored batiks or solid-colored fabrics for blocks and fourth border

1¾ yards of black fabric for sashing, first border, third border, bias tubing, and circle appliqués

1⅔ yards of multicolored print for second border and binding

2½ yards of fabric for backing

44" x 56" piece of batting

Scraps of template plastic and cardboard

Paper-piecing foundation material

Cutting

From the assorted pastel-colored fabrics, cut a *total* of:

27 strips, 1½" x 22". Set aside the leftover fabrics for the paper-pieced blocks.

From the black fabric, cut:

1 piece, 36" x 42"; cut into ⅞"-wide bias strips to total approximately 560" when pieced together

11 strips, 1½" x 42"; crosscut 8 strips into:
    6 rectangles, 1½" x 10½"
    4 strips, 1½" x 20½"
    2 strips, 1½" x 34½"
    2 strips, 1½" x 32½"

Set aside the leftover fabric for the circle appliqués.

From the *lengthwise grain* of the multicolored print, cut:

4 strips, 5½" x 54"
4 binding strips, 2" x 54"
4 squares, 2½" x 2½"

Making the Stained Glass Blocks

Refer to "Paper Foundation Piecing" (page 7) to trace nine copies of the Stained Glass block pattern (page 23) onto your paper-piecing foundation material. Construct the blocks, following the given sewing order and using a variety of the remaining assorted pastel colored fabrics in each block.

Assembling the Quilt Top

1. Arrange the blocks into three rows of three blocks each, rotating every other block 180° for variety. Label the position of each block (i.e. row 1, center).

2. Refer to "Bias-Strip Tubing" (page 14) to make approximately 560" of ¼"-wide continuous bias tubing from the black bias strips. Refer to "Appliquéd Circles" (page 14) to make 28 circles from the remaining black fabric.

3. Referring to the block placement guides and the photo (page 26), use the bias tubing to create the wrought-iron design on each block. Thread baste the tubing in place temporarily, and then permanently attach

Quilt finished size: 38" x 50"

Block: Stained Glass • **Block finished size:** 6" x 10"

it using your favorite appliqué technique. Appliqué circles to the ends of each design. Set aside the remaining eight circles for the second border design.

Center block placement guide

Upper-left- and lower-right-corner block placement guide

Lower-left- and upper-right-corner block placement guide

Top/bottom block placement guide

Side block placement guide

4. Alternately join the blocks in each row with two black 1½" x 10½" sashing rectangles. Press the seam allowances toward the sashing rectangles.

Make 2.

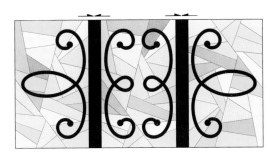

Make 1.

5. Refer to the quilt assembly diagram (page 28) to alternately join the block rows and the black 1½" x 20½" sashing strips. Press the seam allowances toward the sashing strips. Sew black 1½" x 34½" first-border strips to the sides of the quilt top. Press the seam allowances toward the first-border strips.

6. Refer to "Borders with Mitered Corners" (page 16) to add the multicolored floral 5½"-wide second-border strips to the quilt top. Press the seam allowances toward the second border.

7. Sew the black 1½" x 32½" third-border strips to the top and bottom of the quilt top. Join the three 1½" x 42" strips together end to end to make one long strip. From the pieced strip, cut two strips, 1½" x 46½", and sew them to the sides of the quilt top. Press the seam allowances toward the third border.

8. To assemble the pieced fourth border, stitch nine assorted pastel 1½" x 22" strips together along the long edges. Press the seam allowances in one direction. Repeat to make a total of three strip sets. Crosscut the strips sets into 20 segments, 2½" wide.

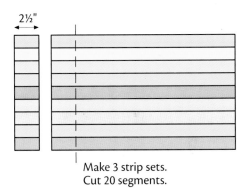

2½"

Make 3 strip sets.
Cut 20 segments.

9. Stitch five segments together end to end. Remove one unit from one of the remaining segments and stitch it to the end of the pieced five-segment strip. Repeat to make a total of two side borders. Sew these strips to the sides of the quilt top. Press the seam allowances toward the black third border. Stitch four segments together end to end. Remove two units from one end to make a 34-unit strip. Sew multicolored floral 2½" squares to both ends of the strip. Repeat to make a total of two strips. Sew these strips to the top and bottom of the quilt top. Press the seam allowances toward the black third border.

10. Referring to the placement guide and the photo (page 26), use the remaining bias tubing and circle appliqués to appliqué the wrought-iron design in each corner of the second border.

Border placement guide

Finishing the Quilt

Refer to "Happy Endings" (page 17) as needed.

1. Layer the quilt top with batting and backing; baste.

2. Quilt as desired.

3. Square up the quilt top.

4. Add a rod pocket if desired and bind the quilt with the multicolored floral 2"-wide strips.

5. Stitch a label to the quilt back.

Quilt assembly

Autumn's Harvest

Choose a beautiful multicolored floral or theme print, add strips and strings of homespun plaids, and build a quilt that salutes your favorite season of the year. This quilt is a two-block quilt that alternates string-pieced Handy Andy Variation blocks with string-pieced Hourglass blocks, creating wonderful diagonal lines across the surface.

Materials

Yardages are based on 42"-wide fabrics.

4¼ yards of tan tone-on-tone print for block backgrounds, first and third border corner squares, and second border

3½ yards *total* of assorted homespun fabrics for blocks

3⅓ yards of multicolored floral or theme print for blocks and fourth border

2 yards of variegated red fabric for blocks, first and third borders, fourth border corner squares, and binding

5½ yards of fabric for backing

74" x 93" piece of batting

Paper-piecing foundation material

Cutting

From the tan tone-on-tone print, cut:

11 strips, 2¾" x 42"; crosscut into 152 squares, 2¾" x 2¾"

From the *lengthwise grain* of the remaining tan tone-on-tone print, cut:

3 strips, 4½" x 108"; crosscut into:
    2 strips, 4½" x 54"
    2 strips, 4½" x 70"
    8 squares, 1½" x 1½"

1 strip, 11" x 108"; crosscut into 9 squares, 11" x 11".
    Cut each square twice diagonally to yield 36 triangles
    (you will have 2 triangles left over).

7 strips, 1¾" x 108"; crosscut into:
    72 rectangles, 1¾" x 6"
    152 squares, 1¾" x 1¾"

From the *lengthwise grain* of the multicolored floral or theme print, cut:

4 strips, 6½" x 108"; crosscut into:
    2 strips, 6½" x 80"
    2 strips, 6½" x 60"

7 strips, 2" x 108"

From the *lengthwise grain* of the variegated red fabric, cut:

10 strips, 1½" x 65"

7 strips, 2" x 65"; crosscut 2 strips into 64 squares, 2" x 2".
    Set aside the remainder of the strips for the binding.

1 strip, 6½" x 65"; crosscut into 4 squares, 6½" x 6½".
    From the remainder of the strip, cut 2 strips, 2" x 39";
    crosscut into 30 squares, 2" x 2".

Making the Blocks

1. From the assorted homespun prints, cut a variety of 1½"- to 2"-wide strips for the string-pieced portions of each block.

2. Using the patterns (pages 32–37) and referring to "Paper Foundation Piecing" (page 7), trace 18 copies of the Handy Andy Variation block pattern, 17 copies of the Hourglass block pattern, and 4 copies of the second-border corner pattern onto your paper-piecing foundation material.

3. Refer to the given fabric key and sewing order and use the precut fabric pieces as follows to construct each block:

   For the Handy Andy blocks, use the variegated red 2" squares for piece 1 in each part. Use the tan 1¾" x 6" rectangles for pieces A12, C2, C3, D12 and the tan 1¾" squares for pieces 2 and 3 of parts A, B, D, and E. Use the tan 2¾" squares for pieces 5 and 6 of parts A, B, D, and E.

   For the Hourglass blocks, use the triangles cut from the tan 11" squares for pieces A6 and B6. Use the floral print 2"-wide strips in the string-pieced areas.

   For the second-border corner squares, use the remainder of the variegated red 2" squares for piece 1, the remainder of the tan 1¾" squares for pieces 2 and 3, and the remainder of the tan 2¾" squares for pieces 5 and 6.

Quilt finished size: 69" x 87"

Blocks: Handy Andy Variation and Hourglass

Block finished size: 9" x 9"

Assembling the Quilt Top

1. Refer to the quilt assembly diagram to alternately arrange the blocks into seven rows of five blocks each. Make sure the Hourglass blocks are rotated correctly in each row. Sew the blocks in each row together. Press the seam allowances toward the Hourglass blocks. Sew the rows together. Press the seam allowances open.

2. Measure the quilt top through the center from top to bottom and trim two of the variegated red 1½" x 65" strips to this measurement for the side borders. Measure the quilt top through the center from side to side and cut two of the remaining red strips to this measurement for the top and bottom borders. Sew the side borders to the sides of the quilt top. Press the seam allowances toward the borders. Add tan 1½" squares to both ends of the top and bottom borders. Sew these strips to the top and bottom of the quilt top. Press the seam allowances toward the borders.

3. Repeat step 2 to add the tan 4½"-wide strips to the quilt top for the second border, using the border corner squares at both ends of the top and bottom borders. Press the seam allowances toward the first border. Add the variegated red 1½"-wide strips to the quilt top in the same manner for the third border, piecing the strips together as necessary to achieve the required length for the side borders and using the remaining tan 1½" squares at the ends of the top and bottom borders. Press the seam allowances toward the third border. Add the floral print 6½"-wide strips to the quilt top in the same manner for the fourth border, adding the variegated red 6½" squares to both ends of the top and bottom borders. Press the seam allowances toward the fourth border.

Finishing the Quilt

Refer to "Happy Endings" (page 17) as needed.

1. Layer the quilt top with batting and backing; baste.

2. Quilt as desired.

3. Square up the quilt top.

4. Add a rod pocket if desired, and bind the quilt with the remaining variegated red 2"-wide binding strips.

5. Stitch a label to the quilt back.

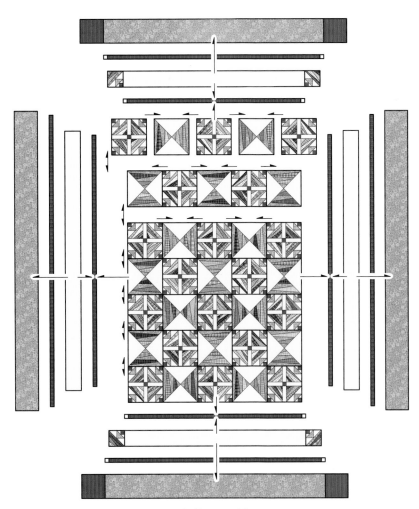

Quilt assembly

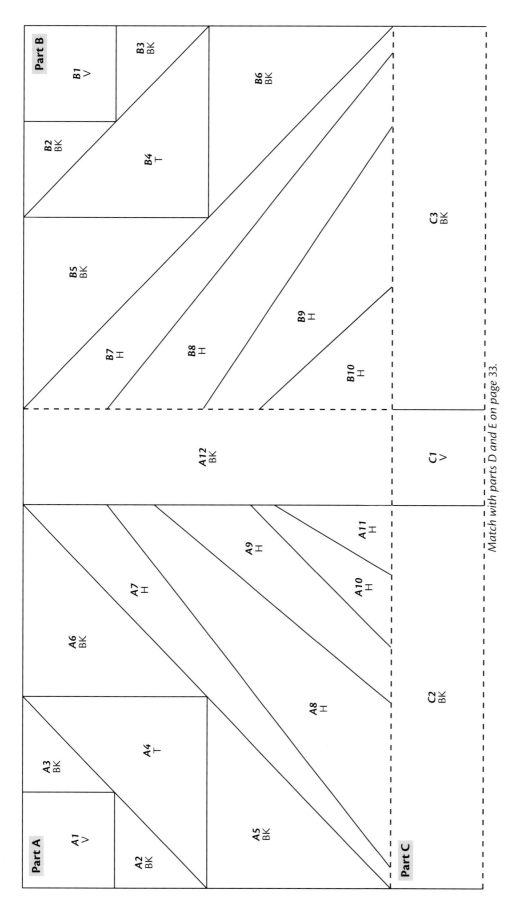

Match with parts D and E on page 33.

Part B

B1 V
B3 BK
B2 BK
B4 T
B6 BK
B5 BK
B7 H
B8 H
B9 H
B10 H
C3 BK

A12 BK
C1 V

A6 BK
A7 H
A9 H
A11 H
A10 H
A8 H
C2 BK

Part A
A3 BK
A4 T
A1 V
A2 BK
A5 BK

Part C

**Handy Andy Variation Block
Foundation Pattern**
Parts A, B, and C

Fabric Key
V—Variegated red stripe
BK—Background
H—Homespun
T—Theme/floral print

Sewing Order
Piece each part in
numerical order.*
Join A to B (AB).
Join AB to C (ABC).
Join D to E (DE).
Join ABC to DE (ABCDE).

*For variety, homespun strings
can be added or deleted for
pieces 7–10 or 11.*

**Handy Andy Variation Block
Foundation Pattern**
Parts D and E

Fabric Key

V—Variegated red stripe
BK—Background
H—Homespun
T—Theme/floral print

Sewing Order

Piece each part in
numerical order.*
Join A to B (AB).
Join AB to C (ABC).
Join D to E (DE).
Join ABC to DE (ABCDE).

*For variety, homespun strings
can be added or deleted for
pieces 7–10 or 11.*

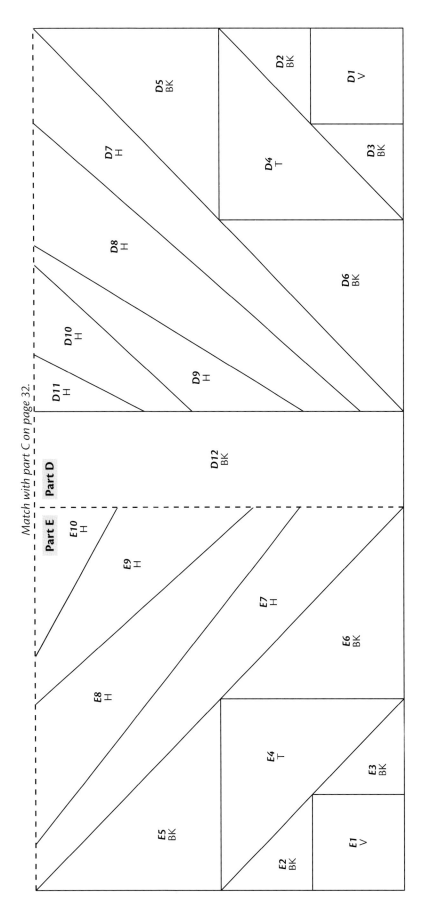

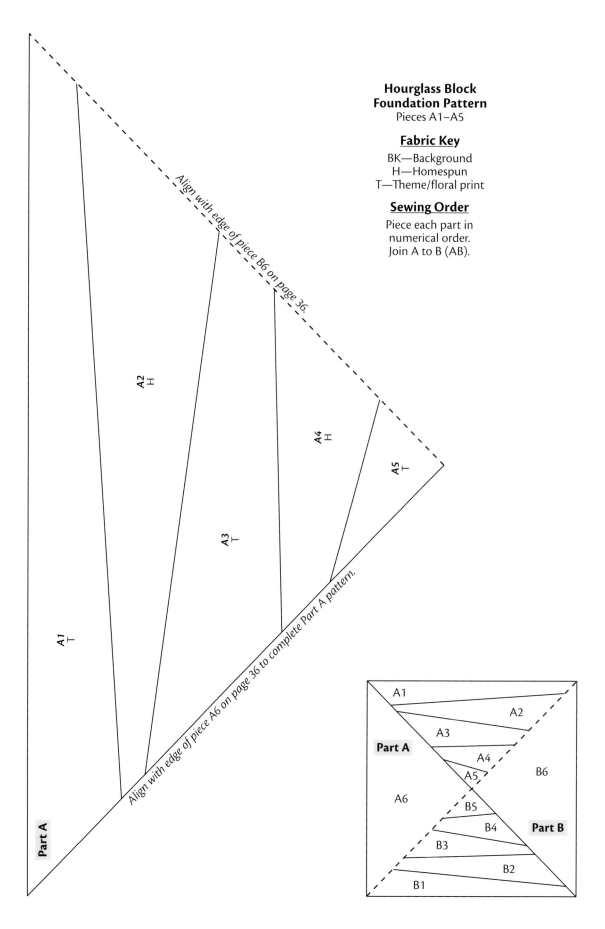

**Hourglass Block
Foundation Pattern**
Pieces A1–A5

Fabric Key

BK—Background
H—Homespun
T—Theme/floral print

Sewing Order

Piece each part in
numerical order.
Join A to B (AB).

Align with edge of piece B6 on page 36.

Align with edge of piece A6 on page 36 to complete Part A pattern.

A2
H

A4
H

A5
T

A3
T

A1
T

Part A

A1
A2
A3
A4
A5
B6
Part A
A6
B5
B4
Part B
B3
B2
B1

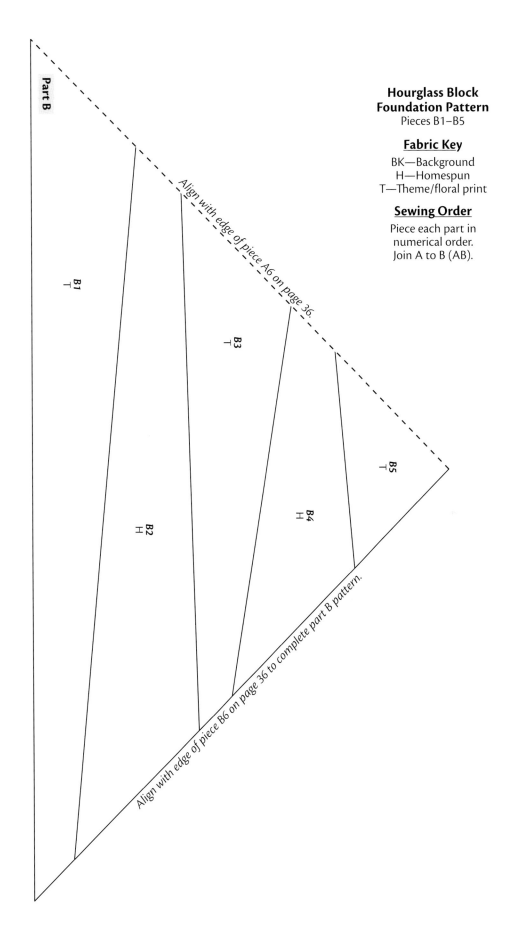

**Hourglass Block
Foundation Pattern**
Pieces B1–B5

Fabric Key

BK—Background
H—Homespun
T—Theme/floral print

Sewing Order

Piece each part in
numerical order.
Join A to B (AB).

Part B

B1
T

Align with edge of piece A6 on page 36.

B3
T

B5
T

B4
H

B2
H

Align with edge of piece B6 on page 36 to complete part B pattern.

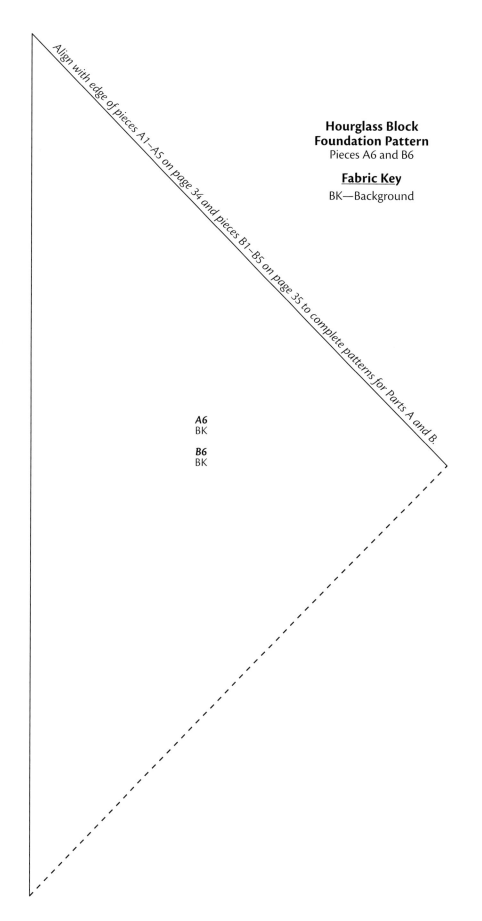

Align with edge of pieces A1–A5 on page 34 and pieces B1–B5 on page 35 to complete patterns for Parts A and B.

**Hourglass Block
Foundation Pattern**
Pieces A6 and B6

Fabric Key
BK—Background

A6
BK

B6
BK

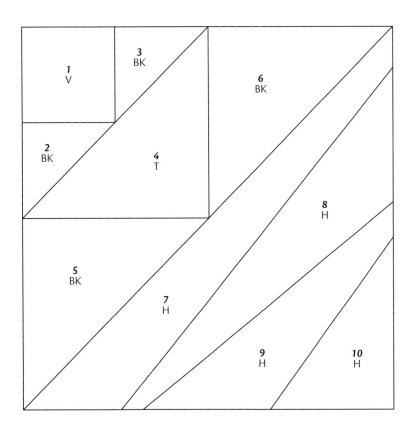

**Second-Border Corner-Square
Foundation Pattern**

Fabric Key

V—Variegated stripe
BK—Background
H—Homespun
T—Theme/floral print

Sewing Order

Piece each pattern in
numerical order.*

*For variety, homespun strings
can be added or deleted for pieces 7–10.*

Floral View

Perhaps you, too, can't resist the beautiful floral prints that are so abundantly available and seem to be calling out "Buy me! Buy me!" Each fabric is so wonderful to touch—but just too marvelous to cut. Well, here's a quilt design that lets you use "just one strip" of many, many floral prints! The design suggests a glorious blue sky that showcases beautiful flowers outside your window. Breathe deeply, imagine the fragrances, and enjoy!

Materials

Yardages are based on 42"-wide fabrics.

3" x 12" piece *each* of 38 assorted light floral prints for blocks

3" x 12" piece *each* of 38 assorted dark floral prints for blocks

1 yard of sky print for blocks and second border

1 yard of dark green leaf print for blocks and binding

⅔ yard of wood-grain print for blocks, first border, and third border

2⅞ yards of fabric for backing

44" x 62" piece of batting

Paper-piecing foundation material

Cutting

From the wood-grain print, cut:
9 strips, 1½" x 42"
4 strips, 2" x 42"

From the sky print, cut:
4 strips, 4½" x 42"
2 strips, 5" x 42"; crosscut into 16 squares, 5" x 5". Cut each square once diagonally to yield 32 triangles.

From the dark green leaf print, cut:
7 strips, 2" x 42"; crosscut 2 strips into 40 squares, 2" x 2". Set aside the remaining strips for the binding.
3 strips, 5" x 42"

Making the Blocks

1. Using the patterns (pages 41–46) and referring to "Paper-Foundation Piecing" (page 7), trace 8 copies of the Flying Darts Variation block pattern; 14 copies of the A border pattern; 2 copies *each* of the B, C, and E border patterns; and 4 copies of the D border pattern onto your paper-piecing foundation material.

2. Refer to the given fabric key and sewing order and use the precut fabric pieces as follows to construct each block:

   For the Flying Darts Variation blocks, use the green 2" squares for piece 1 of each part, the sky print triangles for piece 5 of parts A, B, D, and E, and the wood-grain 2"-wide strips for pieces A6, C2, C3, and D6. Use different light and dark floral prints in each part.

   For the border blocks, use the green print 5"-wide strips for the dark green areas.

Assembling the Quilt Top

1. Refer to the quilt assembly diagram to arrange the Flying Darts Variation blocks into four horizontal rows of two blocks each. Rotate the blocks so that a dark floral print is next to a light floral print. Sew the blocks in each row together. Press the seam allowances open. Sew the rows together. Press the seam allowances open.

2. Refer to "Borders with Butted Corners" (page 15) to add the wood-grain 1½"-wide first border strips to the quilt top. Press the seam allowances toward the borders. Repeat with the sky print 4½"-wide borders for the second border, pressing the seam allowances toward the first border. Use the remaining wood-grain 1½"-wide strips to add the third border in the same manner. Press the seam allowances toward the third border.

Quilt finished size: 38" x 56"

Blocks and finished sizes:

Flying Darts Variation: 9" x 9" • Border Block A: 4" x 8"

Border Blocks B, C, and D: 4" x 4" • Border Block E: 4" x 6"

3. To make the fourth border, sew the border blocks together as shown. Refer to the quilt assembly diagram to stitch the top and bottom borders to the quilt top. Press the seam allowances toward the third border. Join the side borders to the sides of the quilt top. Press the seam allowances toward the third border.

Finishing the Quilt

Refer to "Happy Endings" (page 17) as needed.

1. Layer the quilt top with batting and backing; baste.

2. Quilt as desired.

3. Square up the quilt top.

4. Add a rod pocket if desired and bind the quilt with the green leaf print 2"-wide strips.

5. Stitch a label to the quilt back.

Top/bottom border.
Make 2.

Side border.
Make 2.

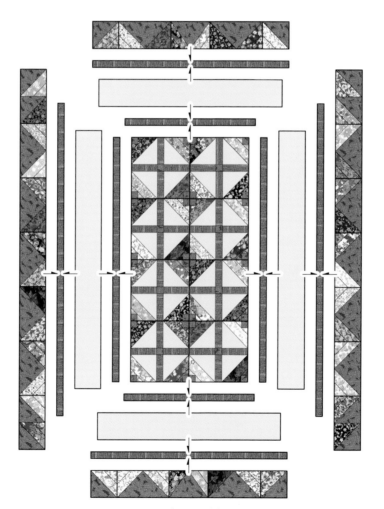

Quilt assembly

Flying Darts Variation Block Foundation Pattern

Fabric Key

DF1—Dark floral print 1
DF2—Dark floral print 2
G—Dark green leaf print
LF1—Light floral print 1
LF2—Light floral print 2
S—Sky print
W—Wood grain print

Sewing Order

Piece each part in
numerical order.
Join A to B (AB).
Join AB to C (ABC).
Join D to E (DE).
Join ABC to DE (ABCDE).

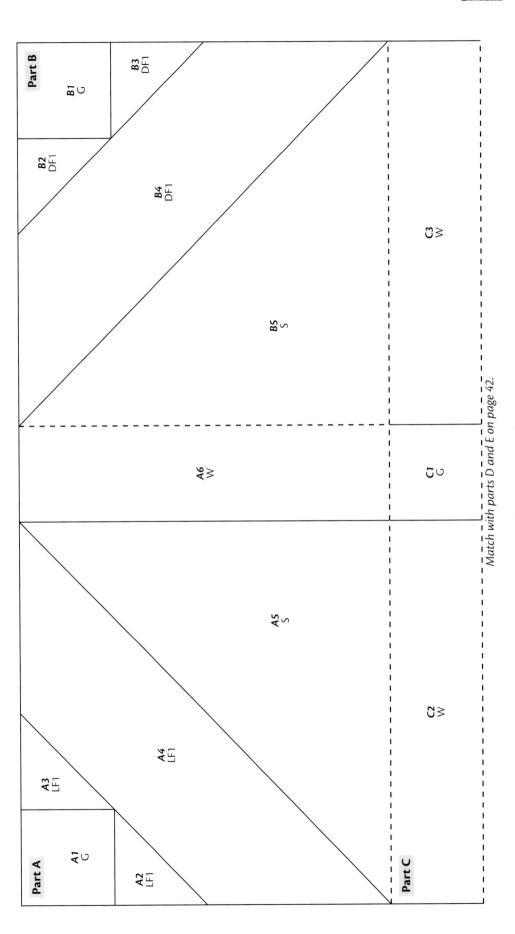

Match with parts D and E on page 42.

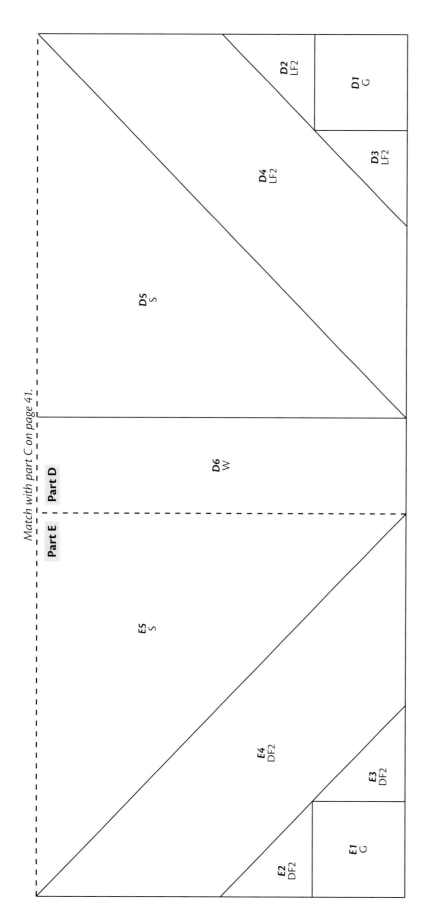

Match with part C on page 41.

Part D

Part E

D1
G

D2
LF2

D3
LF2

D4
LF2

D5
S

D6
W

E5
S

E4
DF2

E3
DF2

E2
DF2

E1
G

Flying Darts Variation Block
Foundation Pattern

Fabric Key

DF1—Dark floral print 1
DF2—Dark floral print 2
G—Dark green leaf print
LF1—Light floral print 1
LF2—Light floral print 2
S—Sky print
W—Wood grain print

Sewing Order

Piece each part in
numerical order.
Join A to B (AB).
Join AB to C (ABC).
Join D to E (DE).
Join ABC to DE (ABCDE).

**Border Block A
Foundation Pattern**

Fabric Key

F1—Floral print 1*
F2—Floral print 2*
G—Dark green print

*If you have larger pieces
of the floral prints, combine
pieces 2 and 3 and pieces 4 and 5.*

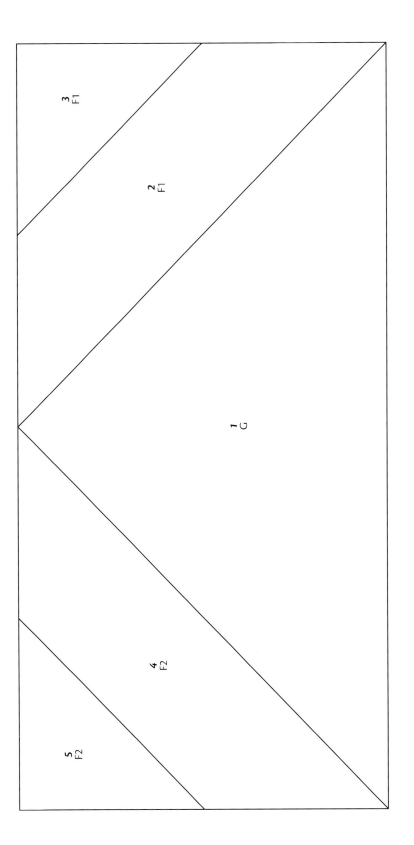

43

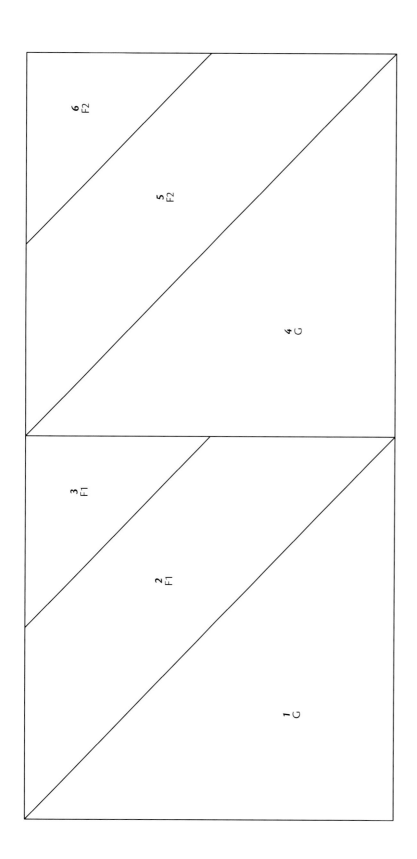

**Border Block B
Foundation Pattern**

Fabric Key

F1—Floral print 1*
F2—Floral print 2*
G—Dark green print

*If you have larger pieces
of the floral prints, combine
pieces 2 and 3 and pieces 5 and 6.*

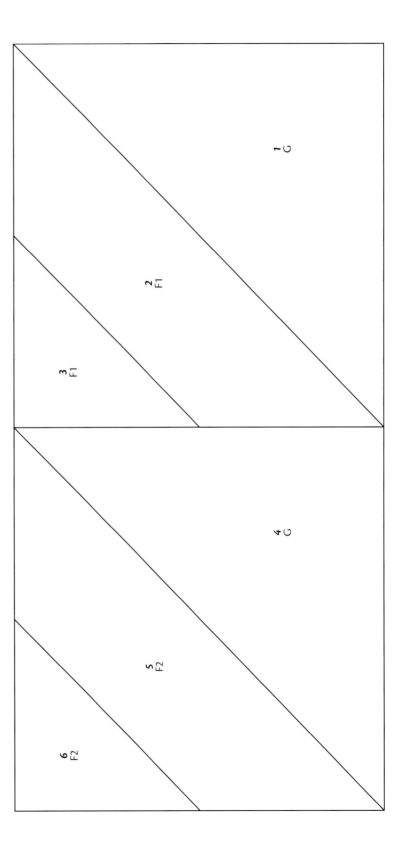

**Border Block C
Foundation Pattern**

Fabric Key

F1—Floral print 1*
F2—Floral print 2*
G—Dark green print

*If you have larger pieces
of the floral prints, combine
pieces 2 and 3 and pieces 5 and 6.*

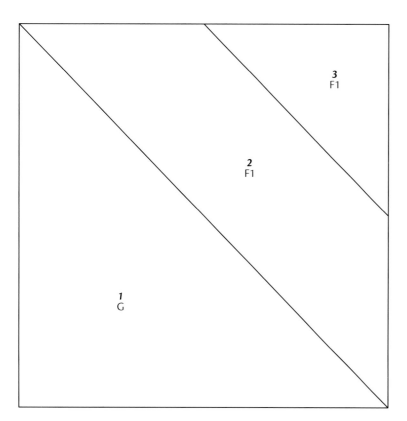

**Border Block A
Foundation Pattern**

Fabric Key

F1—Floral print 1*
F2—Floral print 2*
G—Dark green print

*If you have larger pieces
of the floral prints, combine
pieces 2 and 3 and pieces 4 and 5.*

Block D

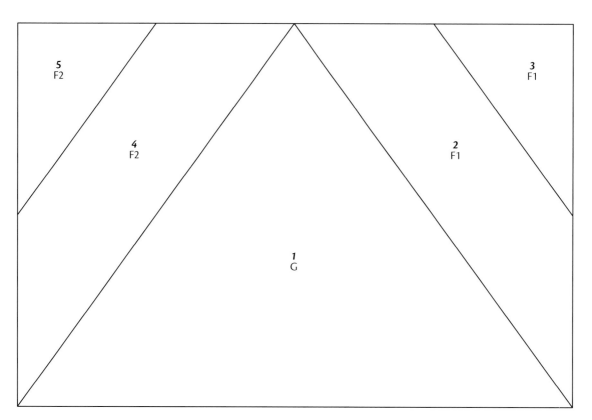

Block E

46

Bow-Tied Bouquets

Many of us collect 1930s reproduction fabrics, those cute novelty-print fabrics with little characters and tiny flowers, but don't know what to do with them once we get them home. By combining pieced Bow Tie blocks, Necktie blocks, and appliquéd floral bouquets, this quilt makes use of those fabrics and also attracts those of us who enjoy a bit of appliqué.

Materials

Yardages are based on 42"-wide fabrics.

6⅛ yards of white fabric for block backgrounds, first border, third border, and fifth border

¼ yard *each* of 24 assorted 1930s reproduction prints for blocks, first border, and fifth border

2¼ yards of green fabric 1 for bias-tube ribbons, second and fourth borders, and binding

⅔ yard of green fabric 2 for bias-tube vines and stems

¼ yard *total* of assorted green scraps for leaves

7 yards of fabric for backing

84" x 108" piece of batting

1¼ yards of 17"-wide paper-backed fusible web

427 precut ½" hexagon templates (see page 96)

Cutting

From the white fabric, cut:
4 strips, 14" x 42"; crosscut into 7 squares, 14" x 14"
21 strips, 3½" x 42"; crosscut into:
    10 pieces, 3½" x 12½"
    192 squares, 3½" x 3½"

From the *lengthwise grain* of the remaining white fabric, cut:
4 strips, 9½" x 72"

From green fabric 1, cut:
24 strips, 2" x 42". You will use 14 strips for the second and fourth borders and 10 strips for the binding.
⅞"-wide *bias* strips to total approximately 370"

From green fabric 2, cut:
⅝"-wide *bias* strips to total approximately 511"

From *each* of the 24 assorted reproduction prints, cut 1 set of squares with each set consisting of:
8 squares, 3½" x 3½" (192 total; you will have 4 left over)
8 squares, 2" x 2" (192 total)

Making the Necktie Blocks

1. Choose eight sets of reproduction print squares.

2. Using a sharp pencil or fabric marker, lightly draw a diagonal line from corner to corner on the wrong side of each reproduction print 2" square.

3. With right sides together, position a marked square in the upper right corner of a white 3½" square. Sew on the marked line. Trim ¼" from the stitching. Press the seam allowances toward the print triangle. Repeat with the remaining squares.

Make 8 sets
of 8 units each.

4. Sew each reproduction print 3½" square to a unit from step 3 of the same print. Press the seam allowances toward the print squares.

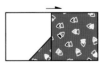

Make 8 sets
of 8 units each.

Quilt finished size: 78" x 102"

Blocks and finished sizes:

Bow Tie: 6" x 6" • **Necktie:** 12" x 12" • **Bouquet:** 12" x 12"

5. Sew two matching units from step 4 together as shown. Press the seam allowance open. Repeat to make a total of eight sets of four units each.

Make 8 sets
of 4 units each.

6. Arrange four matching units from step 5 into two rows of two blocks each as shown. Sew the units in each row together. Press the seam allowances open. Sew the rows together. Press the seam allowances open. Repeat to make a total of eight Necktie blocks.

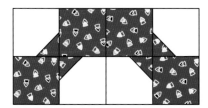

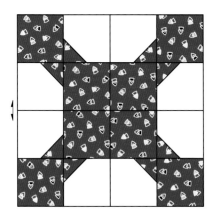

Necktie block.
Make 8.

Making the Appliqué Pieces

1. Refer to "English-Paper-Pieced Hexagon Units" (page 12) to construct 61 seven-piece flowers from the leftover reproduction prints. For each flower, use one print for the center hexagon and one print for the outer hexagons.

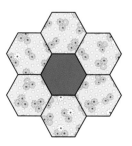

Make 61.

2. Refer to "Bias-Strip Tubing" (page 14) to make ¼"-wide bias tubing from the green fabric 1 bias strips for the bows. You will need 13 lengths approximately 28" long; join pieces as necessary to make the required length. Also make ⅛"-wide bias tubing from the green fabric 2 bias strips for the stems. Lengths in several sizes will be needed for the blocks and the third border, but the joined ends can be covered by flowers and leaves.

3. Using the pattern (page 52), trace 107 leaves on the paper side of the fusible web, leaving at least ¼" between each leaf. Roughly cut around each pattern. Follow the manufacturer's instructions to fuse the shapes to the wrong side of the assorted green scraps. Cut out each leaf on the lines.

Appliquéing the Bouquet Blocks

1. Fold each white 14" square in half, and then in half again. Lightly finger-press the folds to mark the square center.

2. Refer to the placement diagram to pin the green 2 bias stems in place on the right side of a white square using the center marks as a guide. Remove the paper backing from 35 leaves. Add the leaves, and then the flowers to the arrangement. When you are pleased with the arrangement, carefully remove the flowers. Follow the manufacturer's instructions to fuse the leaves in place. Appliqué the stems in place using the desired method. Machine stitch around each leaf using matching thread and a blanket stitch, satin stitch, or straight stitch. Return the flowers to the arrangement and use your preferred method to appliqué them in place. Arrange and appliqué a bow bias-tubing strip in place where shown. Repeat to make a total of seven Bouquet

blocks, reversing the arrangement on three blocks. Set aside the remaining flowers, leaves, and bias-tubing strips for the third border.

Make 4.

Make 3.

3. Carefully press each block. Remove the paper templates from behind each hexagon flower. Square up each background square to 12½" x 12½", keeping the bouquets centered.

Assembling the Quilt Top

1. Refer to the assembly diagram (page 52) to alternately arrange the Necktie blocks and Bouquet blocks into five rows of three blocks each. Move them around and audition them until you are happy with the balance of color. Note the location of the reverse Bouquet blocks.

Join the blocks in each row. Press the seam allowances toward the Bouquet blocks.

2. From six sets of reproduction print squares, take two 3½" squares and two 2" squares. Repeat step 3 of "Making the Necktie Blocks" (page 47) to sew each of the 2" squares to the corners of a white 3½" square. Sew two matching units and the 3½" squares of the same print together as shown.

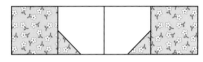

Make 6.

3. Sew the units from step 2, the white 3½" x 12½" pieces, and four different reproduction print 3½" squares from any of the remaining sets together as shown below to make the pieced first border strips. Press the seam allowances as indicated. Add the side borders to the sides of the quilt top. Press the seam allowances toward the quilt center. Add the top and bottom borders to the quilt top. Press the seam allowances toward the quilt center.

4. Refer to "Borders with Butted Corners" (page 15) to add the 2"-wide green 1 strips to the quilt top for the second border, piecing the strips together as needed. Press the seam allowances toward the second border.

5. Fold each of the white 9½"-wide strips in half lengthwise and crosswise; lightly crease the folds to mark the centers. Repeat step 4 to add the borders to the quilt top, trimming the strips as needed and making sure the border and quilt top centers match. Press the seam allowances toward the second border, being careful not to press out the center creases. Add the 2"-wide green 1 fourth border strips to the quilt top in the same manner, piecing the strips together as needed. Press the seam allowances toward the fourth border.

6. Referring to the placement guides (page 51) and step 2 of "Appliquéing the Bouquet Blocks" (page 49), appliqué the third border strip, using the remaining bias tubing, leaves, and hexagon flowers. Remove the paper templates from behind each flower after all of the pieces have been stitched in place.

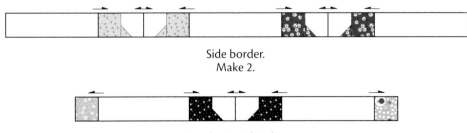

Side border.
Make 2.

Top/bottom border.
Make 2.

7. Refer to steps 2–5 of "Making the Necktie Blocks" (pages 47 and 49) and use the remaining sets of squares of reproduction prints to make 52 Bow Tie blocks. Set aside the remaining pieces in each set for the corner pieces.

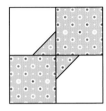

Make 52.

8. From the remaining reproduction print and white squares, make the corner pieces for the fifth border. For each of the four corners you will need one reproduction print 3½" square, two matching 2" squares, and three white 3½" squares. You will also need the matching Bow Tie block.

9. From the pieces you gathered in step 8, refer to step 2 of "Making the Necktie Blocks" (page 47) to sew a reproduction print 2" square to one corner of a white 3½" square. Repeat to make a total of two units. Sew one unit to a matching reproduction print 3½" square as shown to make half block A. Sew the remaining unit to a white 3½" square as shown to make half block B. Repeat with the remaining two prints, arranging the units as shown to make half blocks C and D.

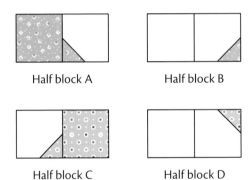

Half block A   Half block B

Half block C   Half block D

10. Refer to the assembly diagram (page 52) to sew 14 Bow Tie blocks together end to end to make the left side border, rotating every other block 90°. Add a C half block to the top of the strip and an A half block to the bottom of the strip. Repeat to make one additional border strip. Sew these strips to the sides of the quilt top, flipping the right side border so it is a mirror image of the left side border. Press the seam allowances toward the fourth border.

11. Refer to the assembly diagram to sew 12 Bow Tie blocks together end to end to make the top border, making sure you place the Bow Tie blocks that match the half blocks at the top of the side borders at the ends. Be careful to position the blocks so they are going in the correct direction, rotating every other block 90°. Add the matching B and D half blocks to the ends of the strip. Sew the strip to the top of the quilt top. Repeat to add the bottom border to the bottom of the quilt top. Press the seam allowances toward the fourth border.

Finishing the Quilt

Refer to "Happy Endings" (page 17) as needed.

1. Layer the quilt top with batting and backing; baste.

2. Quilt as desired.

3. Square up the quilt top.

4. Add a rod pocket if desired and bind the quilt with the 2"-wide green 1 strips.

5. Stitch a label to the quilt back.

Side border placement guide

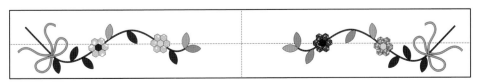

Top/bottom border placement guide

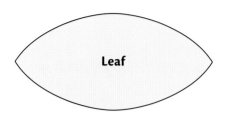

Leaf

Quilt assembly

Miniature Bow Ties and Hexagons

If you think this quilt is too pretty to be a table runner covered up with plates, bowls, and silverware, it would also look great hanging on the wall. Its small size makes it perfect to give as a gift, as well. Whatever you decide, choose your colors to shout, "Happy Valentine's Day," Happy Thanksgiving," "Merry Christmas," or do as I did here—make it a quilt for all seasons.

Materials

Yardages are based on 42"-wide fabrics.

1½ yards of light print for background, borders, and binding

⅔ yard *total* of at least 12 assorted batiks for blocks, hexagons, and middle border

1½ yards of fabric for backing

28" x 52" piece of batting

58 precut ½" hexagon templates (see page 96)

Cutting

From the *lengthwise grain* of the light print, cut:

5 strips, 3½" x 48"; crosscut 2 strips into 24 squares, 3½" x 3½"; set aside the remaining strips for the outer border

3 strips, 1¼" x 48"

8 strips, 2" x 48"; crosscut 4 strips into 84 squares, 2" x 2"; set aside the remaining strips for the binding

From the assorted batiks, cut a *total* of 24 sets of squares, with each set cut from the same fabric and consisting of:

2 squares, 2" x 2" (48 total)
2 squares, 1¼" x 1¼" (48 total)

From the remainder of the assorted batiks, cut a *total* of:

36 squares, 2" x 2"
Set aside the remaining fabric for the hexagons.

Making the Bow Tie Blocks

1. Using a sharp pencil or fabric marker, lightly draw a diagonal line from corner to corner on the wrong side of each batik 1¼" square.

2. With right sides together, position a marked square in the upper-right corner of a light print 2" square. Sew on the marked line. Trim ¼" from the stitching. Press the seam allowance toward the batik triangle. Repeat to make a total of 48 units.

Make 48.

3. Stitch a matching batik 2" square to each unit from step 2. Press the seam allowances toward the batik squares.

Make 48.

4. Sew two matching units from step 3 together as shown. Press the seam allowance open. Repeat to make a total of 24 Bow Tie blocks.

Make 24.

Quilt finished size: 22½" x 46½"

Block: Bow Tie

Block finished size: 3" x 3"

Assembling the Quilt Top

1. Refer to the assembly diagram to arrange the Bow Tie blocks and light print 3½" squares into 12 rows. Pay careful attention to the orientation of each block. Move the blocks around and audition them in different positions until you are happy with the balance of color. When joining a block to a background square, press the seam allowance toward the background square. When joining two blocks or two background squares, press the seam allowance open. Join the rows. Press the seam allowances open.

2. Refer to "Borders with Butted Corners" (page 15) to add the light print 1¼"-wide inner-border strips to the quilt top, adding the top and bottom borders first, and then the sides. Press the seam allowances toward the border.

3. Alternately stitch together 13 light print 2" squares and 14 batik 2" squares. Press the seam allowances toward the batik squares. Repeat to make a total of two side middle-border strips. In the same manner, stitch together 5 light print 2" squares and 4 batik 2" squares to make two top/bottom middle-border strips.

Side border.
Make 2.

Top/bottom border.
Make 2.

4. Sew the top and bottom pieced borders to the top and bottom edges of the quilt top. Press the seam allowances toward the inner border. Join the side pieced borders to the sides of the quilt top. Press the seam allowances toward the inner border.

5. Repeat step 2 to add the light print 3½"-wide outer borders to the quilt top. Press the seam allowances toward the outer border.

6. Refer to "English-Paper-Pieced Hexagon Units" (page 12) to construct two 13-piece hexagon units and eight 4-piece hexagon units from the leftover batik fabrics. Use the same fabric for the hexagons in each unit.

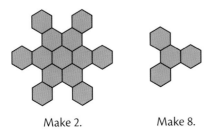

Make 2.   Make 8.

7. Refer to the photo at left to arrange the hexagon units on the quilt top. Using your preferred method and thread that matches the hexagons, appliqué each unit in place. Remove the paper templates from behind each hexagon unit.

Finishing the Quilt

Refer to "Happy Endings" (page 17) as needed.

1. Layer the quilt top with batting and backing; baste.

2. Quilt as desired.

3. Square up the quilt top.

4. Add a rod pocket if desired and bind the quilt with the light print 2"-wide strips.

5. Stitch a label to the quilt back.

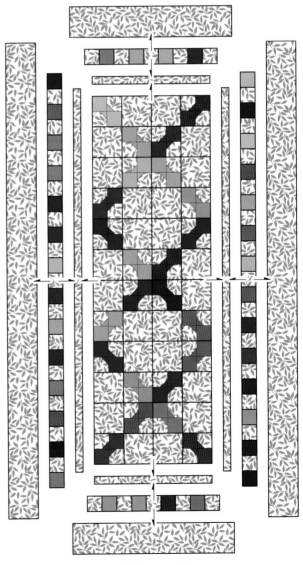

Quilt assembly

Flying in Formation

This quilt consists of a vertical arrangement of Flying Geese blocks separated by sashing strips made of a glorious daisy border print. It's easy to make—and what a visual impact it will have on any bed.

Materials

Yardages are based on 42"-wide fabrics. Choose your border print or theme print first! Then select three different colors to make the rows of Flying Geese. For the "goose" triangle of the Flying Geese blocks, choose two dominant colors from your theme print (in this case I used green and gold). Then choose the background fabric for your Flying Geese blocks. Because my fabric was a different color on each side of the print, I used two colors (blue and tan). For ease in identifying the pieces for the Flying Geese blocks, I've called for the same fabric colors that I used.

5½ yards of border print or theme print for vertical sashing and fifth border*

2 yards of light fabric to coordinate with border or theme print for second border and binding

1⅝ yards *total* of assorted blue prints for Flying Geese block backgrounds

1½ yards *total* of assorted green prints for Flying Geese blocks

1¼ yards *total* of assorted gold prints for Flying Geese blocks

1 yard of brown print for first and third borders

⅔ yard *total* of assorted tan prints for Flying Geese block backgrounds

7 yards of fabric for backing

86" x 108" piece of batting

* Yardage is based on being able to cut four border strips and six sashing strips, each 6" wide, from one length of fabric. The amount may vary according to the number of design repetitions across the width of fabric.

Cutting

Patterns for templates A–D are on page 60.

From the assorted green prints, cut:
177 template A pieces

From the assorted gold prints, cut:
142 template A pieces

From the assorted tan prints, cut:
175 template B pieces

From the assorted blue prints, cut:
144 template B pieces
319 template B reversed pieces
4 template D pieces
4 template D reversed pieces

From the *lengthwise grain* of the theme print, cut:
6 strips, 6" x 70½". If you are using a border print, be sure to center the design in each strip; you may need to adjust the width of the strips depending upon the width of the design.
2 strips, 5½" x 84"
2 strips, 5½" x 108"

From the brown print, cut:
17 strips, 1½" x 42"; cut *1* strip into four pieces, 1½" x 10½"
4 squares, 3½" x 3½"
2 template C pieces

From the coordinating light fabric, cut:
8 strips, 5½" x 42"
9 binding strips, 2" x 42"

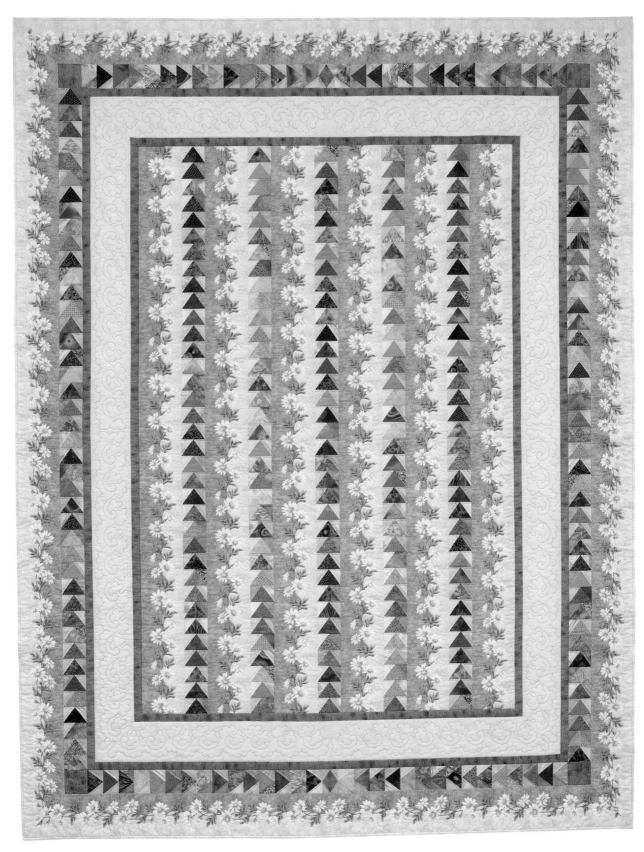

Quilt finished size: 78" x 100"

Block: Flying Geese

Block finished size: 3" x 2"

Making the Flying Geese Blocks

Use the template A, B, and B reversed pieces to make Flying Geese blocks in the color combinations shown.

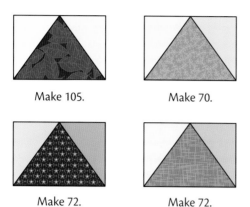

Make 105.   Make 70.

Make 72.   Make 72.

Assembling the Quilt Top

1. Set aside the Flying Geese blocks with blue B and B reversed pieces for the fourth border. Join the remaining green blocks into three vertical rows of 35 blocks each. Join the remaining gold blocks into two rows of 35 blocks each. Make sure all of the "geese" are pointing in the same direction.

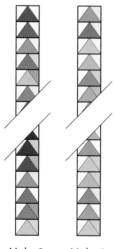

Make 3.   Make 2.

2. Refer to the quilt assembly diagram (page 59) to alternately join the block strips and theme print 6" x 70½" sashing strips. If your theme print strips are a different color on each half of the design like the print used in the featured quilt, make sure the background of the block strips abuts the same color on the sashing strips. Press the seam allowances toward the sashing strips.

3. Join two brown print 1½" x 42" strips end to end. Repeat to make a total of eight pieced strips. Add brown print 1½" x 10½" pieces to both ends of two of the pieced strips. Sew two coordinating light print 5½" x 42" strips together end to end. Repeat to make a total of four pieced strips. Press all of the seam allowances open.

4. With the seam lines centered, make border strip units as shown. Press the seam allowances away from the light border strips.

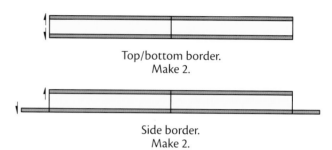

Top/bottom border.
Make 2.

Side border.
Make 2.

5. Measure the quilt top for borders as described in "Borders with Mitered Corners" (page 16). Cut the border strip units to fit, keeping the seam lines centered. Stitch the border units to the quilt top, mitering the corners. Press the seam allowances toward the first border.

6. Using the Flying Geese blocks with the blue B and B reversed pieces and referring to the quilt assembly diagram, alternately join 21 green blocks and 21 gold blocks along the long edges, beginning with a green block and ending with a gold block. Make sure all of the blocks are pointing in the same direction. Stitch this border to the left side of the quilt top. Make sure the geese are pointing toward the top of the quilt. Press the seam allowance toward the third border. Repeat to make one additional border strip, but begin with a gold block and end with a green block. Stitch this border to the right-hand side of the quilt top. Again, make sure the geese are pointing toward the top of the quilt.

7. From the remaining Flying Geese blocks, alternately join eight green blocks and seven gold blocks along the long edges, beginning and ending with a green block. Make sure all of the blocks are pointing in the same direction. Repeat to make a total of two strips. In the same manner, join eight gold blocks and seven green blocks, beginning and ending with a gold block. Make a total of two strips.

8. Sew the C, D, and D reversed pieces together to make two border center units.

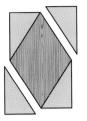 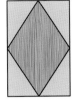

Make 2.

9. Referring to the assembly diagram, sew the border strips from step 7 and the units from step 8 together to make the top and bottom borders. Make sure the geese are pointing toward the center unit and that the colors alternate on each strip. Add brown 3½" squares to both ends of each border strip. Press the seam allowances toward the squares. Sew the borders to the top and bottom edges of the quilt top. Press the seam allowances toward the third border.

10. Measure the quilt top for borders as described in "Borders with Mitered Corners." Trim the 5½"-wide theme print strips to these measurements and stitch them to the quilt top, mitering the corners. Press the seam allowances toward the fifth border.

Finishing the Quilt

Refer to "Happy Endings" (page 17) as needed.

1. Layer the quilt top with batting and backing; baste.

2. Quilt as desired.

3. Square up the quilt top.

4. Add a rod pocket if desired and bind the quilt with the coordinating light fabric 2"-wide strips.

5. Stitch a label to the quilt back.

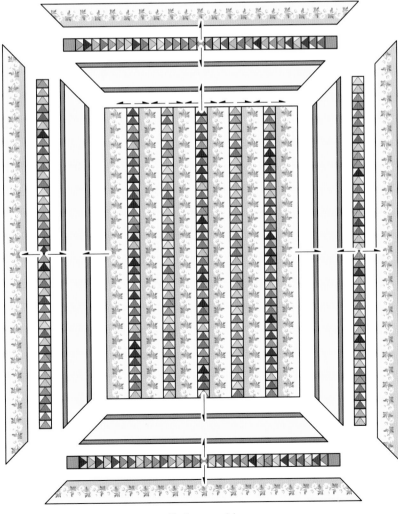

Quilt assembly

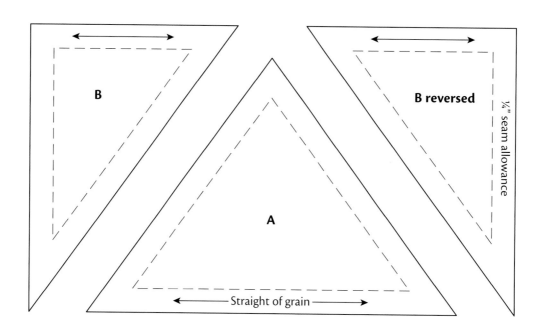

B

B reversed

¼" seam allowance

A

Straight of grain

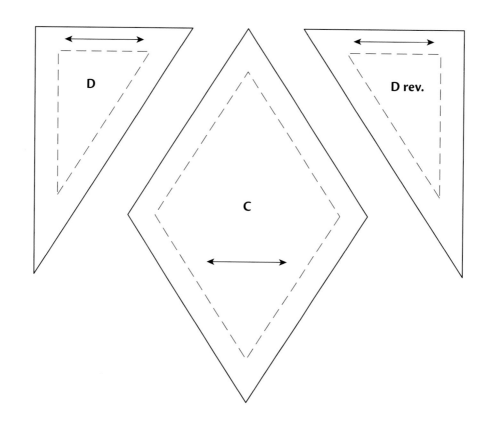

D

D rev.

C

Pinwheel Stars

Do you hate to throw away even the tiniest bits of fabric? Do you collect the leftover scraps from your friends' quilting projects? Do you love to purchase those packets of quilting fabric charm squares but never know what to do with them when you get home? If you answered "yes" to any of these questions, this quilt is truly for you. Gather up all those precious fabric scraps and begin piecing these Elongated Pinwheel blocks.

Materials

Yardages are based on 42"-wide fabrics.

8⅓ yards *total* of assorted scraps for blocks

4⅓ yards *total* of at least 10 assorted light fabrics for blocks

2½ yards of multicolored print for outer border and binding

⅝ yard of brown print for inner border

½ yard of light print for middle border

5 yards of fabric for backing

75" x 90" piece of batting

Paper-piecing foundation material

Cutting

From *each* of the 10 assorted light fabrics for blocks, cut:
1 rectangle, 5½" x 7½" (10 total). Set aside the remainder of the fabric for the paper-pieced blocks.

From the brown print, cut:
7 strips, 2½" x 42"

From the light print for middle border, cut:
8 strips, 1½" x 42"

From the *lengthwise grain* of the multicolored print, cut:
4 strips, 4½" x 80"
4 binding strips, 2" x 80"

Making the Blocks

Refer to "Paper Foundation Piecing" (page 7) to trace 100 copies of the Elongated Pinwheel block pattern (page 64) onto your paper-piecing foundation material. Construct the blocks following the given sewing order and using seven different scraps for the string-pieced sections in each block. When joining parts, press the seam allowances toward the background triangles.

Quilt finished size: 69" x 84"

Block: Elongated Pinwheel

Block finished size: 5" x 7"

Assembling the Quilt Top

1. Refer to the assembly diagram (below) to arrange the blocks and the 10 assorted background 5½" x 7½" rectangles into 10 horizontal rows of 11 blocks each. Stitch the blocks in each row together. Press the seam allowances open. Sew the rows together. Press the seam allowances open.

2. Refer to "Borders with Butted Corners" (page 15) to add the brown 2½"-wide inner-border strips to the quilt top, piecing the strips as needed. Press the seam allowances toward the border. Repeat to add the 1½"-wide light print middle-border strips to the quilt top. Press the seam allowances toward the inner border. Sew the multicolored print 4½"-wide outer-

border strips to the quilt in the same manner, trimming the strips to the lengths needed. Press the seam allowances toward the outer border.

Finishing the Quilt

Refer to "Happy Endings" (page 17) as needed.

1. Layer the quilt top with batting and backing; baste.

2. Quilt as desired.

3. Square up the quilt top.

4. Add a rod pocket if desired and bind the quilt with the multicolored 2"-wide strips.

5. Stitch a label to the quilt back.

Quilt assembly

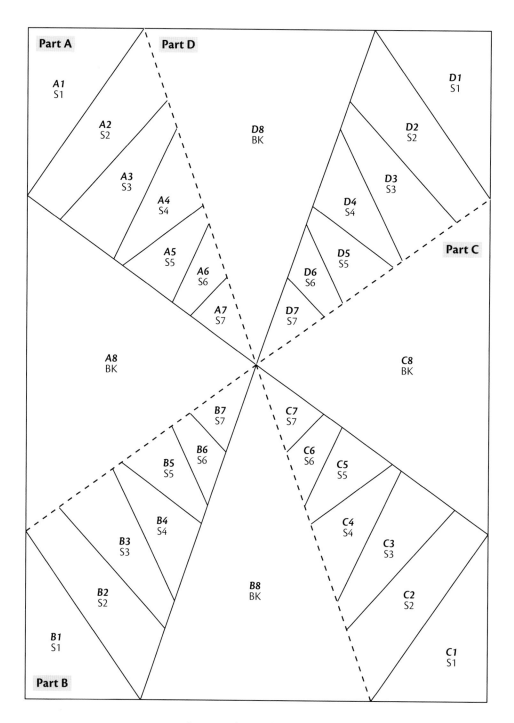

**Elongated Pinwheel Block
Foundation Pattern**

Fabric Key

BK—Background
S1–S7—Scraps of assorted fabrics

Sewing Order

Piece each part in
numerical order.
Join A to B (AB).
Join C to D (CD).
Join AB to CD (ABCD).

Centered and Surrounded

This quilt is really a process of elimination. You take one pieced block (the Elongated Pinwheel) and make different blocks by removing parts, creating what I call partial blocks. The result is a centered block surrounded by a unique frame of partial blocks. The bonus is a large open area for intricate quilting and/or embellishments. The string-pieced areas of the center blocks, as well as the border blocks, are made from two color families. To make your quilt pop, I suggest that one of your color families be brighter and bolder than the other, such as the turquoise I used here. If you don't have lots of scraps, a traditional one-fabric border can be substituted for the string-pieced border blocks.

Materials

Yardages are based on 42"-wide fabrics.

2¼ yards *total* of assorted color 1 (brown) scraps for blocks and fourth border

2 yards of tan print for background and first border

1½ yards of multicolored print for blocks, second border, and binding

¾ yard *total* of assorted color 2 (turquoise) scraps for blocks and fourth border

¼ yard of accent (blue) fabric for third border

3⅛ yards of fabric for backing

53" x 65" piece of batting

Paper-piecing foundation material

Cutting

From the tan print, cut:
2 strips, 8" x 42"; crosscut into 12 rectangles, 6" x 8"
1 strip, 5" x 42", crosscut into 6 rectangles, 5" x 7"
2 strips, 4" x 42"; crosscut into 6 rectangles, 4" x 9"
5 strips, 1½" x 42"
Set aside the leftover fabric for the remaining paper-pieced blocks.

From the multicolored print, cut:
5 strips, 2½" x 42"
4 strips, 4" x 42"; crosscut into 48 rectangles, 3" x 4". Cut each rectangle once diagonally to yield 96 triangles.
6 binding strips, 2" x 42"

From the accent fabric, cut:
5 strips, 1" x 42"

Making the Blocks

1. Using the patterns (pages 69–77) and referring to "Paper Foundation Piecing" (page 7), trace one copy of the Elongated Pinwheel block pattern; two copies *each* of A, A reversed, corner A, corner A reversed, D, D reversed, E, and F; four copies *each* of short E, narrow F, and the border corner square; six copies *each* of B, short B, C, and narrow C; and 18 copies of the border block onto your paper-piecing foundation material.

2. Refer to the fabric key and sewing order to construct each block, using the tan 6" x 8" rectangles for the B and C blocks, the tan 5" x 7" rectangles for the short B blocks, the tan 4" x 9" rectangles for the narrow C blocks, and the multicolored print triangles for the string-pieced sections of the appropriate blocks where indicated on the patterns.

Quilt finished size: 47" x 59"

Blocks and finished sizes:

Elongated Pinwheel: 5" x 7" • Blocks A, B, C, D, E, and F: 5" x 7" • Corner A block: 2½" x 3½"

Short B and short E blocks: 5" x 3½" • Narrow C and narrow F blocks: 2½" x 7"

Border blocks: 5" x 10" • Border corner blocks: 5" x 5"

Assembling the Quilt Top

1. Arrange the blocks into seven rows of seven blocks each as shown below, being sure to rotate the blocks correctly to achieve the design. Sew the bocks in each row together. Press the seam allowances open. Sew the rows together. Press the seam allowances open.

2. Refer to "Borders with Butted Corners" (page 15) and the assembly diagram (page 68) to add the tan print 1½"-wide first border strips to the quilt top, piecing strips together as needed. Press the seam allowances toward the border. Repeat for the multicolored 2½"-wide second border strips and accent fabric 1"-wide third border strips, pressing the seam allowances toward the newly added border each time.

3. Measure the quilt top through the center from top to bottom and from side to side. Make a note of each measurement. Sew five border foundation blocks together end to end, rotating every other one for variety. Press the seam allowances in one direction. Trim the strip to the length measured. Repeat to make a total of two border strips. Sew these strips to the sides of the quilt top.

Make 2.

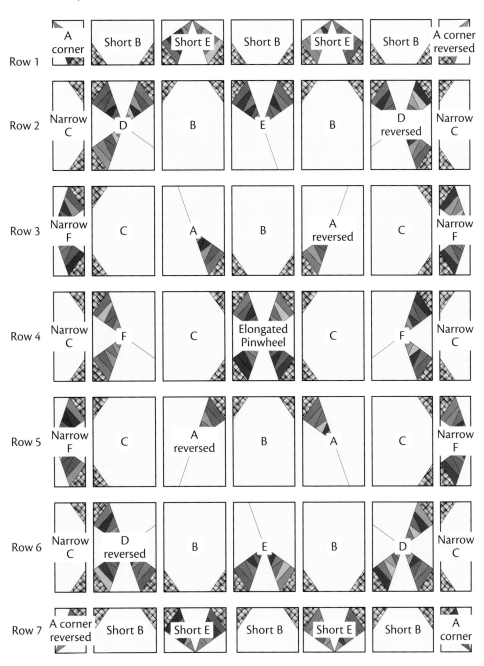

4. Repeat step 3 to join four border foundation blocks together in the same manner. Trim the strip to the width measured. Add a border corner block to the ends of the strip, positioning the blocks so the background fabric is at the top inner corner. Repeat to make a total of two border strips. Sew these strips to the top and bottom edges of the quilt top, being sure to place the strips so the background fabric of the border corner square is next to the third border.

Make 2.

Finishing the Quilt

Refer to "Happy Endings" (page 17) as needed.

1. Layer the quilt top with batting and backing; baste.

2. Quilt as desired.

3. Square up the quilt top.

4. Add a rod pocket if desired and bind the quilt with the multicolored print 2"-wide strips.

5. Stitch a label to the quilt back.

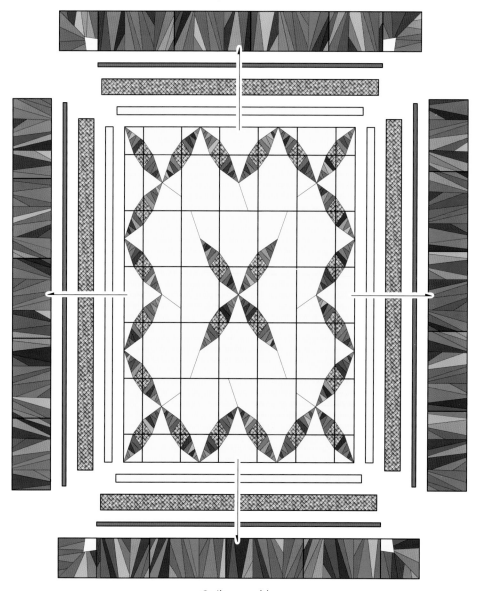

Quilt assembly

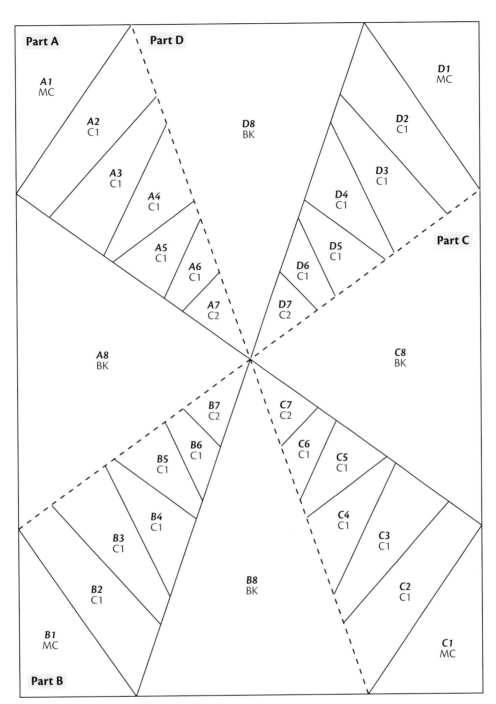

**Elongated Pinwheel Block
Foundation Pattern**

Fabric Key

BK—Background
C1—Color 1 scraps
C2—Color 2 scraps
MC—Multicolored print

Sewing Order

Piece each part in
numerical order.
Join A to B (AB).
Join C to D (CD).
Join AB to CD (ABCD).

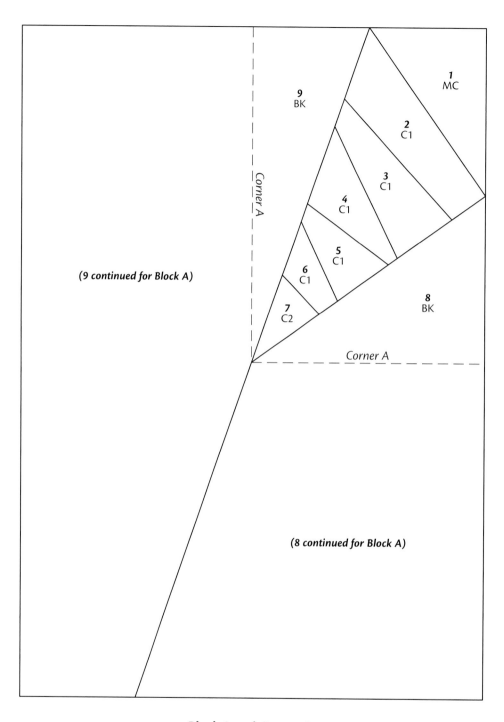

**Block A and Corner A
Foundation Patterns**

Fabric Key

BK—Background
C1—Color 1 scraps
C2—Color 2 scraps
MC—Multicolored print

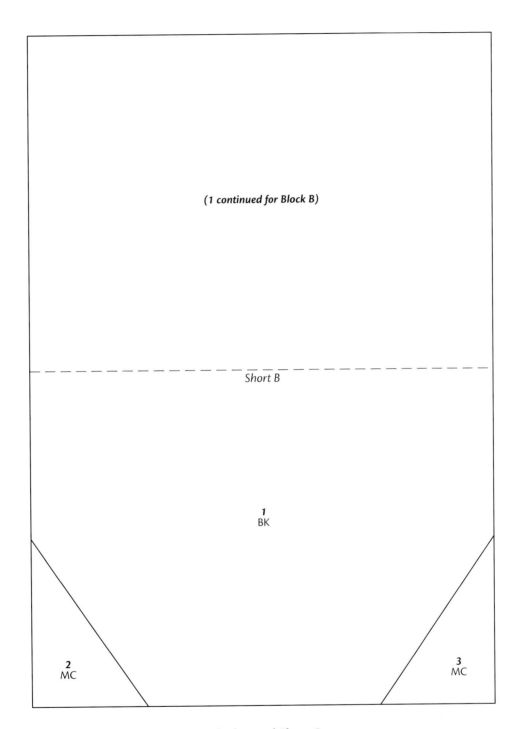

(1 continued for Block B)

Short B

1
BK

2
MC

3
MC

**Block B and Short B
Foundation Patterns**

Fabric Key

BK—Background
MC—Multicolored print

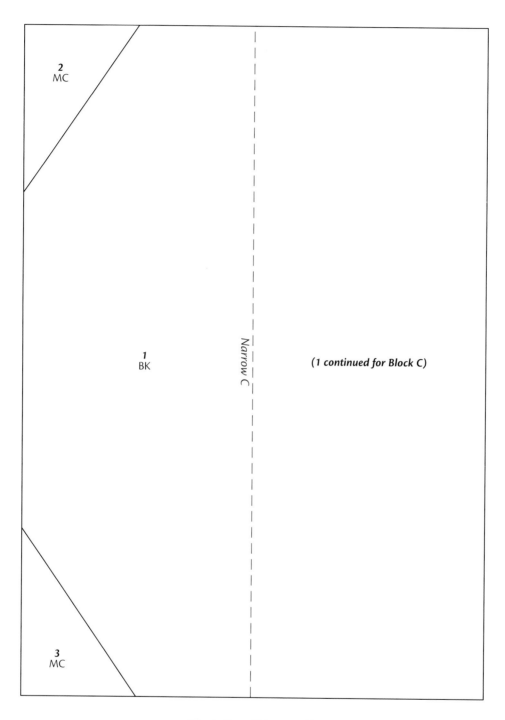

2
MC

1
BK

Narrow C

(*1 continued for Block C*)

3
MC

**Block C and Narrow C
Foundation Patterns**

Fabric Key
BK—Background
MC—Multicolored print

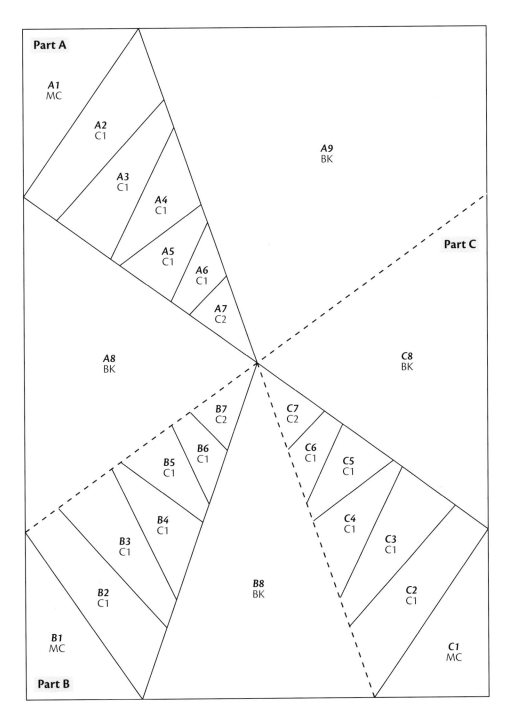

Block D
Foundation Pattern

Fabric Key

BK—Background
C1—Color 1 scraps
C2—Color 2 scraps
MC—Multicolored print

Sewing Order

Piece each part in
numerical order.
Join B to C (BC).
Join A to BC (ABC).

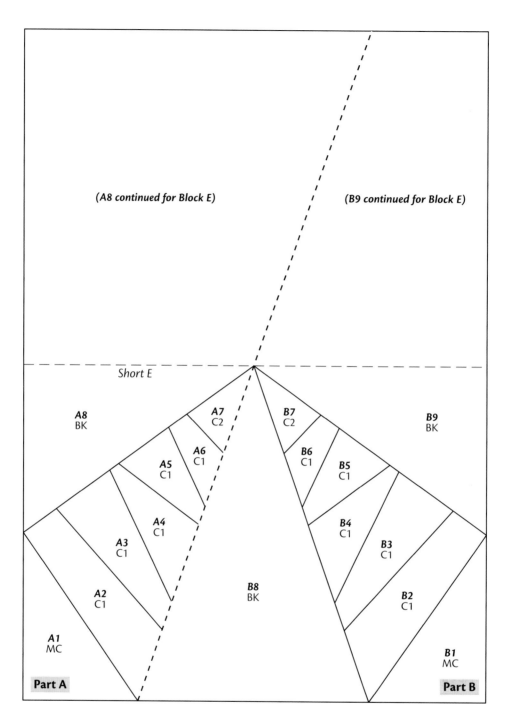

(A8 continued for Block E)   (B9 continued for Block E)

Short E

A8
BK

A7
C2

B7
C2

B9
BK

A6
C1

B6
C1

A5
C1

B5
C1

A4
C1

B4
C1

A3
C1

B3
C1

A2
C1

B8
BK

B2
C1

A1
MC

B1
MC

Part A   **Part B**

Block E and Short E
Foundation Patterns

Fabric Key

BK—Background
C1—Color 1 scraps
C2—Color 2 scraps
MC—Multicolored print

Sewing Order

Piece each part in
numerical order.
Join A to B (AB).

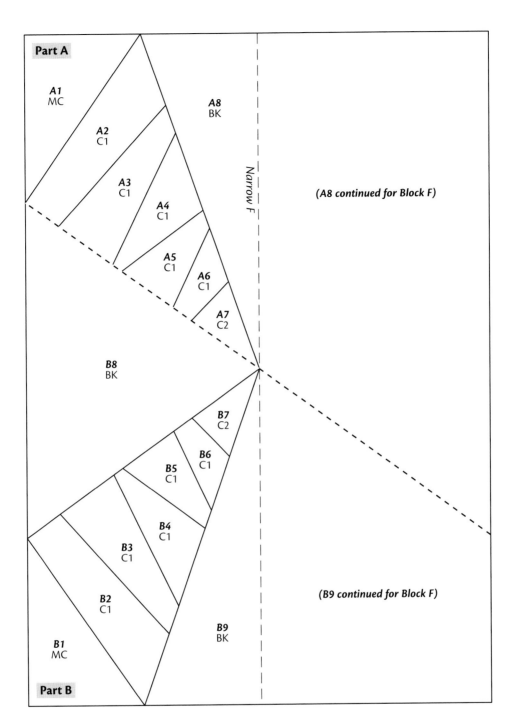

Part A

A1
MC

A2
C1

A3
C1

A4
C1

A5
C1

A6
C1

A7
C2

A8
BK

Narrow F

(A8 continued for Block F)

B8
BK

B7
C2

B6
C1

B5
C1

B4
C1

B3
C1

B2
C1

B1
MC

B9
BK

(B9 continued for Block F)

Part B

Block F and Narrow F
Foundation Patterns

Fabric Key

BK—Background
C1—Color 1 scraps
C2—Color 2 scraps
MC—Multicolored print

Sewing Order

Piece each part in
numerical order.
Join A to B (AB).

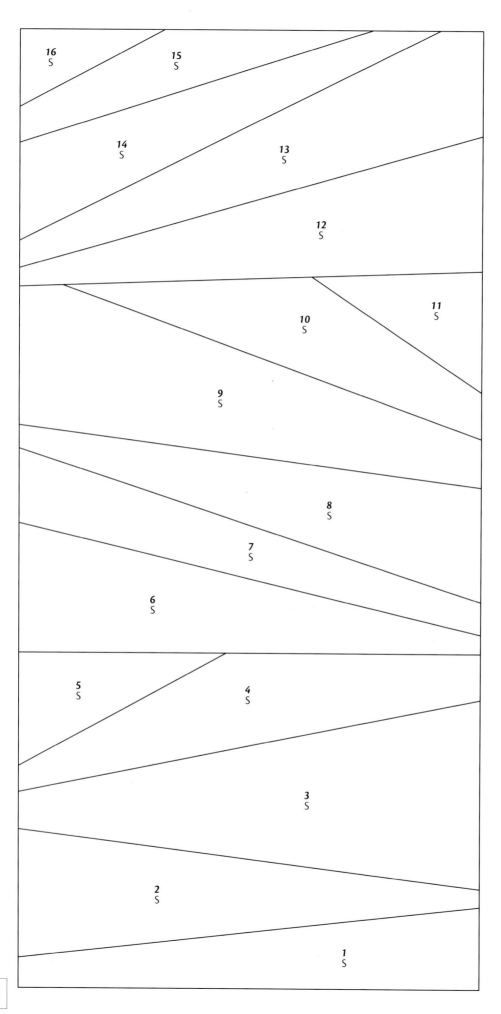

**Border
Foundation Pattern**

Fabric Key
S—Scraps of either
Color 1 or Color 2

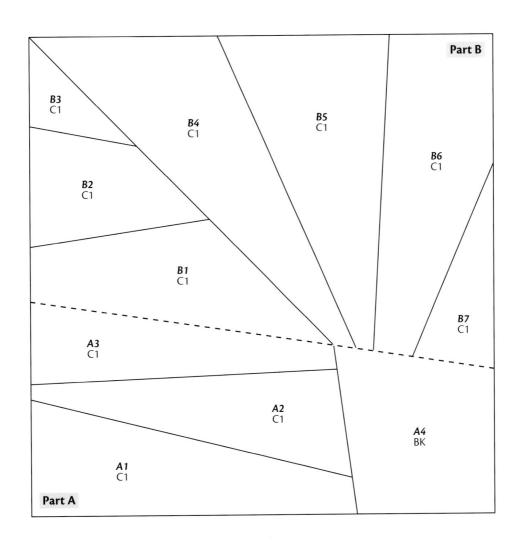

**Border
Foundation Pattern**

Fabric Key

BK—Background
C1—Color 1 scraps

Sewing Order

Piece each part in
numerical order.
Join A to B (AB).

Stand Up for the Red, White, and Blue

Gather up every shade of red, white, and blue fabric scraps that you have, add a dash of gold for punch, and you have the makings of a quilt worth saluting! This quilt uses just one block constructed in two color sets: a blue set and a red set. The overall design comes from careful placement and block rotation.

Materials

Yardages are based on 42"-wide fabrics.

4 yards *total* of assorted cream and white prints for blocks

2⅝ yards of gold print for blocks and inner border

2½ yards *total* of assorted red prints for blocks

2½ yards *total* of assorted blue prints for blocks

1¾ yards of blue print for outer border and binding

7 yards of fabric for backing

86" x 104" piece of batting

Paper-piecing foundation material

Cutting

From the gold print, cut:

19 strips, 3½" x 42"; crosscut into 200 squares, 3½" x 3½". Cut each square once diagonally to yield 400 triangles.

13 strips, 1½" x 42"; crosscut 3 strips into 80 squares, 1½" x 1½"

From the blue outer-border fabric, cut:

10 strips, 3½" x 42"

10 binding strips, 2" x 42"

Making the Blocks

1. Cut the assorted cream and white fabrics, assorted red fabrics, and assorted blue fabrics into 1¾"-wide strips. You will need strips from 2½" long to 9" long.

2. Refer to "Paper Foundation Piecing" (page 7) to trace 80 copies of the Split Geese in the Cabin block pattern (pages 81 and 82) onto your paper-piecing foundation material. Paper piece the blocks in numerical order, following the fabric key. Make 40 blocks using the assorted red print strips as the dark fabric and 40 blocks using the assorted blue print strips as the dark fabric. For all of the blocks, use the gold squares for piece 1 and the gold triangles for the remaining accent pieces, and the white and cream strips for the light fabric.

Assembling the Quilt Top

1. Refer to the quilt assembly diagram (page 80) to arrange the blocks into 10 rows of eight blocks each. Be sure to rotate the blocks and colors correctly to achieve the design. Sew the blocks in each row together. Press the seam allowances in opposite directions from row to row. Stitch the rows together. Press the seam allowances open.

2. Refer to "Borders with Butted Corners" (page 15) to add the gold 1½"-wide inner-border strips to the quilt top. Press the seam allowances toward the border. Repeat with the blue 3½"-wide outer-border strips, pressing the seam allowances toward the outer border.

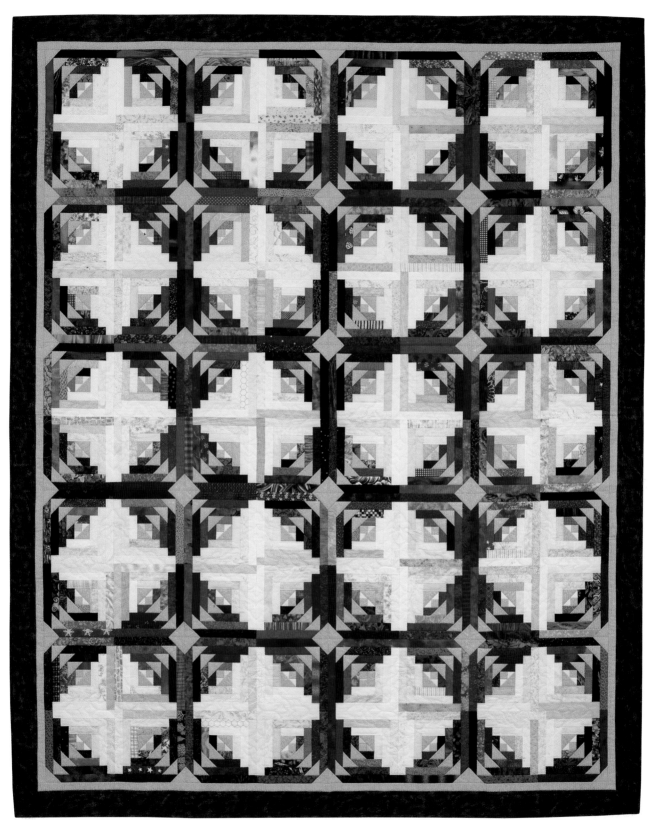

Quilt finished size: 80" x 98"

Block: Split Geese in the Cabin

Block finished size: 9" x 9"

Finishing the Quilt

Refer to "Happy Endings" (page 17) as needed.

1. Layer the quilt top with batting and backing; baste.

2. Quilt as desired.

3. Square up the quilt top.

4. Add a rod pocket if desired and bind the quilt with the blue 2"-wide binding strips.

5. Stitch a label to the quilt back.

Quilt assembly

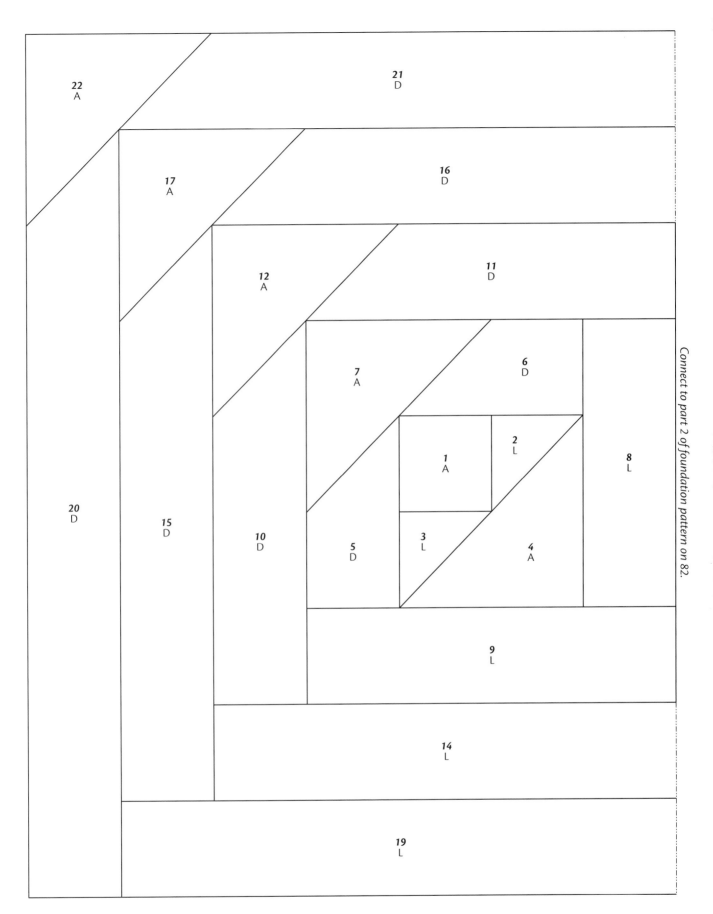

Connect to part 2 of foundation pattern on 82.

**Split Geese in the Cabin Block
Foundation Pattern (part 1)**

<u>Fabric Key</u>
A—Accent fabric
L—Lights
D—Darks

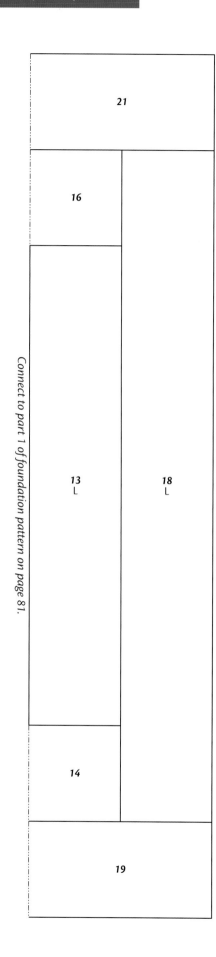

Split Geese in the Cabin Block Foundation Pattern (part 1)

Fabric Key

A—Accent fabric
L—Lights
D—Darks

Connect to part 1 of foundation pattern on page 81.

Civil War Recollections

Calling all you lovers of Civil War–reproduction fabrics and homespun plaids. This quilt is for you! Colorful medium- and dark-value fabrics seem to exude warmth and coziness. The quilt's overall impact is enhanced by reversing the traditional placement of the folded fabric "prairie points" on the outer border, pointing them in instead of out to produce a three-dimensional effect.

Materials

Yardages are based on 42"-wide fabrics.

2½ yards total of assorted medium and dark fabrics for blocks and prairie points

1½ yards of unbleached muslin for blocks and middle border

1⅜ yards of brown fabric (accent) for blocks, inner border, and binding

3 yards of fabric for backing

50" x 50" piece of batting

Paper-piecing foundation material

Cutting

From the assorted medium and dark fabrics, cut a *total* of:
76 squares, 4" x 4"
Set aside the leftover fabrics for the paper-pieced blocks.

From the *lengthwise grain* of the muslin, cut:
14 strips, 1¾" x 48"
4 strips, 3½" x 48"

From the *lengthwise grain* of the brown fabric, cut:
4 strips, 3½" x 45"; crosscut into 40 squares,
    3½" x 3½". Cut each square once diagonally to yield
    80 triangles.
6 strips, 2" x 45"; crosscut 1 strip into 16 squares, 2" x 2".
    Set aside the remaining strips for the binding.
4 strips, 1½" x 45"

Making the Blocks

1. Cut the remainder of the assorted medium and dark fabrics into 1¾"-wide strips. You will need strips from 2½" long to 9" long.

2. Refer to "Paper Foundation Piecing" (page 7) to trace 16 copies of the Split Geese in the Cabin block pattern (pages 81 and 82) onto your paper-piecing foundation material. Paper piece the blocks in numerical order, following the fabric key. Use the brown 2" squares for piece 1, the brown triangles for the remaining accent pieces, the muslin 1¾"-wide strips for the light pieces, and the assorted medium and dark strips for the dark pieces.

Assembling the Quilt Top

1. Refer to the assembly diagram (page 85) to arrange the blocks into four rows of four blocks each as shown. Be sure to rotate the blocks correctly to achieve the design. Sew the blocks in each row together. Press the seam allowances in opposite directions from row to row. Sew the rows together. Press the seam allowances open.

2. Center and sew a brown 1½" x 45" strip to a muslin 3½" x 48" strip. Repeat to make a total of four border-strip units.

Make 4.

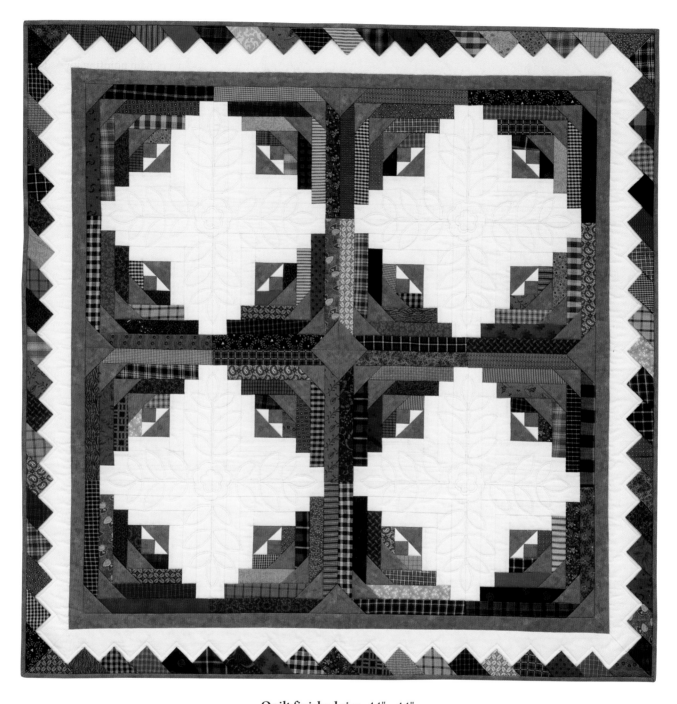

Quilt finished size: 44" x 44"

Block: Split Geese in the Cabin

Block finished size: 9" x 9"

3. Measure the quilt top for borders as described in "Borders with Mitered Corners" (page 16). Cut the border strip units to fit. Stitch the border units to the quilt top, mitering the corners. Press the seam allowances toward the first border. Baste ⅛" from the raw edges.

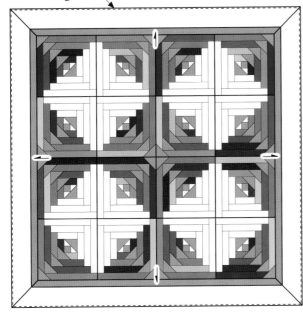

Stabilizing stitch

Quilt assembly

4. Fold each medium or dark 4" square in half diagonally, and then in half diagonally again to form a prairie point.

Make 76.

5. Evenly space 19 prairie points along each side of the quilt top, tucking the folded end of each prairie point into the open end of the next prairie point as shown and aligning the raw edges of each triangle with the

edges of the quilt top. Make sure the corner prairie points align with the mitered seams of the border. Pin each prairie point in place. Machine baste the prairie points to the quilt top, about ⅛" from the raw edge. Note that the prairie points remain pointing inward in this quilt, giving the quilt a more three-dimensional look and feel.

Finishing the Quilt

Refer to "Happy Endings" (page 17) as needed.

1. Layer the quilt top with batting and backing; baste.

2. Quilt as desired.

3. Square up the quilt top.

4. Add a rod pocket if desired and bind the quilt with the brown 2"-wide strips.

5. Hand tack the point of each prairie point to the quilt.

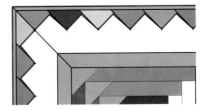

6. Stitch a label to the quilt back.

String Stars

Fabric strings going every direction make this quilt look like it might be challenging, but you simply sew hundreds of scraps together in strip units, and then use templates to cut the units at any angle you'd like. Even the sashing and one of the borders is string pieced. The sky is the limit in terms of colors, prints, stripes, designs, and plaids. Use them all! Simply choose one dominant color in three shades (light, medium, and dark) for the background and borders to tie it all together, and . . . wow!

Materials

Yardage is based on 42"-wide fabrics.

6 yards *total* of assorted fabric scraps and strips at least ¾" wide for blocks, sashing, and first and third borders

1⅔ yards of dark print for fourth border and binding

1⅛ yards of light print for block backgrounds

⅔ yard of medium print for second border

4 yards of fabric for backing

70" x 70" piece of batting

Paper-piecing foundation material

Freezer paper

Cutting

From the light print for block backgrounds, cut:
5 strips, 4½" x 42"; crosscut into 36 squares, 4½" x 4½"
2 strips, 5¼" x 42"; crosscut into 9 squares, 5¼" x 5¼"
    Cut each square twice diagonally to yield 36 triangles.

From the medium print for second border, cut:
6 strips, 3½" x 42"

From the dark print for fourth border and binding, cut:
7 strips, 5½" x 42"
7 binding strips, 2" x 42"

Making the Strip-Pieced Units

1. Cut the assorted fabric scraps into ¾"- to 2"-wide strips. You will need strips that are approximately 20" to 22" long. Trim longer strips to that length and sew shorter strips together to achieve the length needed.

2. Sew the strips together along the long edges in a pleasing arrangement of colors and prints to make a pieced unit that is approximately 10" to 12" wide. Press the seam allowances in one direction. Repeat to make a total of nine pieced units.

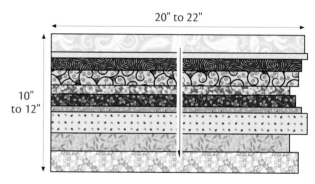

Make 9.

Making the Blocks

1. Using the patterns (page 90), trace nine A squares, 36 B triangles, and 36 C triangles onto the dull side of the freezer paper. Cut out the templates.

2. Place the templates shiny side down on the wrong side of the strip-pieced units, twisting and turning the pieces to achieve greater variety. Leave at least ½" between each template to allow for seam allowance around each piece when cutting. Using a dry iron, press the templates onto the pieced units. Cut out each

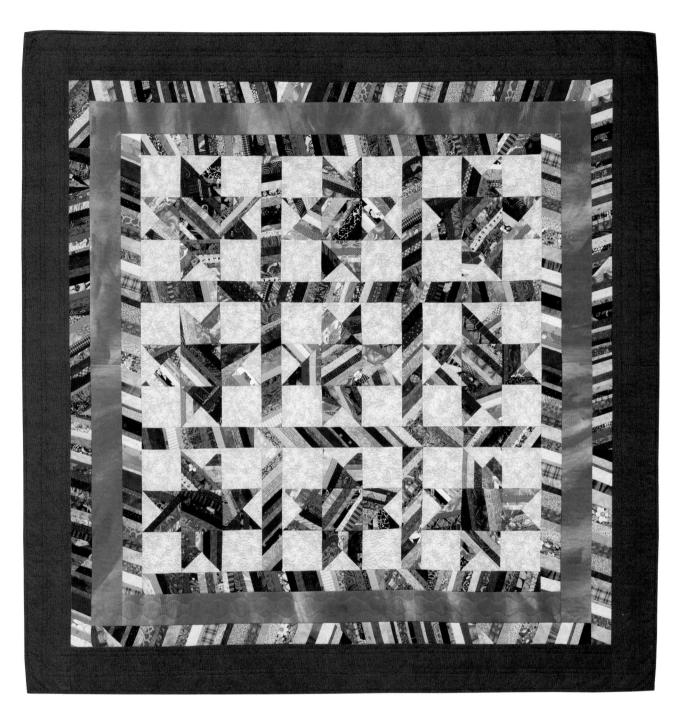

Quilt finished size: 64" x 64"

Block: Twin Star

Block finished size: 12" x 12"

fabric piece, adding a ¼" seam allowance on each side. Do not remove the freezer-paper templates.

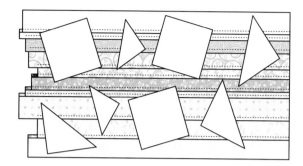

3. Sew a strip-pieced B triangle to a light print triangle, stitching along the freezer-paper template edge. Press the seam allowance toward the light print. Sew a strip-pieced C triangle to this unit, stitching along the freezer-paper edge. Press the seam allowance away from C. Repeat to make a total of 36 star-point units. You may want to "play around" with the units before sewing them together to make sure you have a good mix of colors and prints in each unit.

Make 36.

4. Lay out four light print 4½" squares, four star-point units, and one A square into three rows as shown. Sew the squares in each row together, stitching along the freezer-paper template edges. Press the seam allowances toward the light print squares and the A square. Sew the rows together. Press the seam allowances away from the center row. Repeat to make a total of nine blocks. Remove the freezer-paper templates.

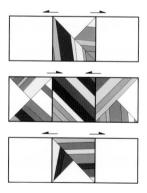 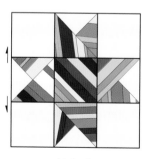

Make 9.

Making the String-Pieced Units

1. Draw six 2" x 12" strips, four 2" x 40" strips, and two 2" x 44" strips on your paper-piecing foundation material. Using a ruler, draw lines across the width of each strip, varying the distance between each line from ¼" to 1½". You can vary the direction of the angles or draw them all going in the same direction. These are the sewing lines. Cut out each strip along the outer lines.

Note: For the longer strips, shorter strips can be drawn and then pieced together to make longer lengths after they are foundation pieced.

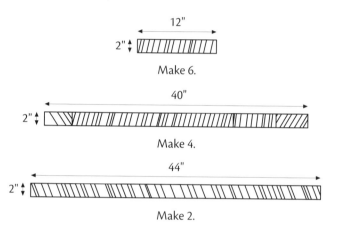

12"

2"

Make 6.

40"

2"

Make 4.

44"

2"

Make 2.

2. Refer to "Paper Foundation Piecing" (page 7) to paper-piece the step 1 foundations, working from one end of each strip to the other. This is a great place to use up small bits of fabric. Pieces should extend at least ¼" on each side and the ends of the foundation material. Trim each strip ¼" from the foundation material.

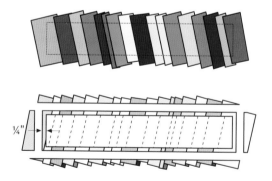

¼"

Assembling the Quilt Top

1. Refer to the assembly diagram (page 89) to arrange the blocks and 2½" x 12½" string-pieced sashing strips into three rows of three blocks and two sashing strips each. Sew the blocks and sashing strips together in each row. Press the seam allowances toward the blocks.

2. Alternately join the block rows and 2½" x 40½" string-pieced horizontal sashing/first-border strips. Press the seam allowances toward the block rows. Sew the 2½" x 44½" string-pieced strips to the sides of the quilt top. Press the seam allowances toward the blocks.

3. Refer to "Borders with Butted Corners" (page 15) to add the medium blue 3½"-wide second border strips to the quilt top, adding the top and bottom borders first, and then the sides; piece the strips as needed. Press the seam allowances toward the second border.

4. Measure the quilt width through the center of the quilt top. Refer to "Making the String-Pieced Units" (page 88) to draw two 2" wide strips the length measured onto your foundation material. Paper piece the strips in the same manner as the previous string-pieced strips. Sew the strips to the top and bottom edges of the quilt top. Press the seam allowances toward the

second border. Measure the quilt length through the center of the quilt top, including the just-added borders. Repeat to make two more string-pieced strips and sew them to the sides of the quilt top.

5. Repeat step 3 to add the dark blue 5½"-wide fourth-border strips to the quilt top. Press the seam allowances toward the fourth border.

Finishing the Quilt

Refer to "Happy Endings" (page 17) as needed.

1. Layer the quilt top with batting and backing; baste.

2. Quilt as desired.

3. Square up the quilt top.

4. Add a rod pocket if desired and bind the quilt with the dark blue 2"-wide strips.

5. Stitch a label to the quilt back.

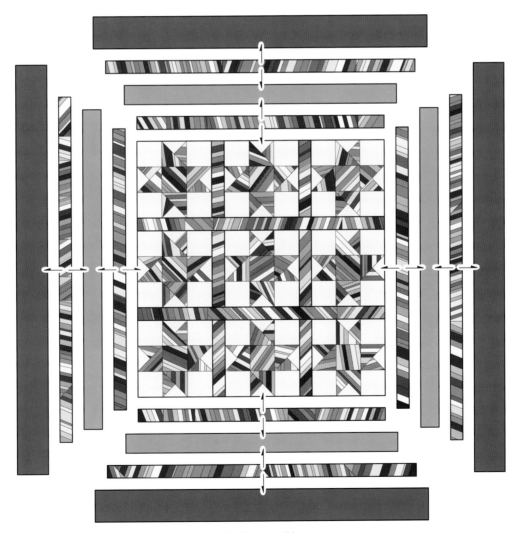

Quilt assembly

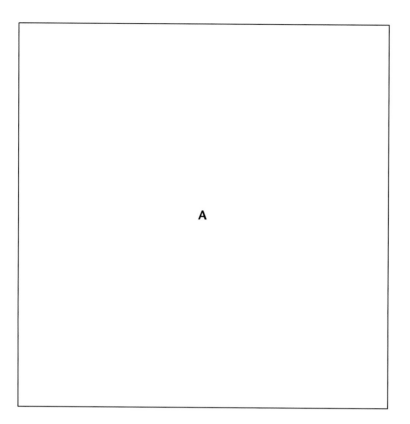

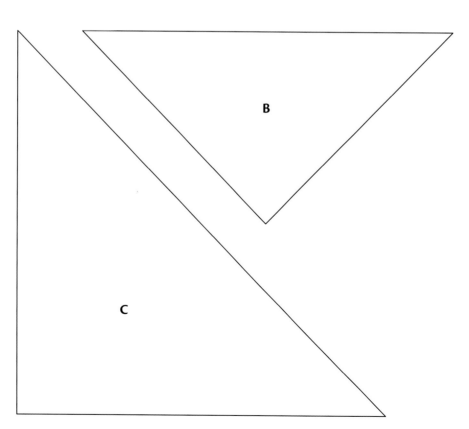

A

B

C

Mardi Gras Nights

Let's dance! Let's sing! Let's celebrate! Bold, bright colors appear even brighter when they're contrasted with black. You can feel the fun and the festivity! This simple four-block quilt is made even more exciting when a series of pieced borders are added.

Materials

Yardages are based on 42"-wide fabrics.

1¾ yards *total* of 18 to 25 assorted bright-colored prints for blocks and second border

1¼ yards of solid black fabric for first border, third border, fifth border, and binding

1⅛ yards *total* or fat eighths (9" x 22") of at least 9 assorted black and dark gray prints for blocks and second border

3 yards of fabric for backing

50" x 50" piece of batting

Paper-piecing foundation material

Cutting

Patterns for templates A and B are on page 94.

From the assorted bright-colored prints, cut a *total* of:
16 template A pieces
16 template B pieces
4 squares, 4½" x 4½"
36 *pairs* of matching squares, 3" x 3" (72 total); cut each square once diagonally to yield 144 triangles
104 rectangles, 2" x 3"

From the assorted black and dark gray prints, cut a *total* of:
16 template A pieces
16 squares, 4½" x 4½"
36 squares, 4" x 4"
4 squares, 2½" x 2½"

From the solid black fabric, cut:
8 strips, 1½" x 42"
6 strips, 2½" x 42"
5 binding strips, 2" x 42"

Making the Twin Star Blocks

1. Sew a bright print A triangle to a black or dark gray A triangle. Press the seam allowance toward the black or gray triangle. Sew a bright print B triangle to this unit. Press the seam allowance toward the B triangle. Repeat to make a total of 16 star-point units.

Make 16.

2. Lay out four black or gray 4½" squares, four star-point units, and one bright print 4½" square into three rows as shown. Sew the squares in each row together. Press the seam allowances toward the bright and black squares. Sew the rows together. Press the seam allowances away from the center row. Repeat to make a total of four blocks.

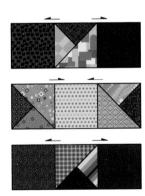 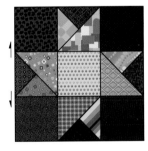

Make 4.

Assembling the Quilt Top

1. Refer to the quilt assembly diagram (page 93) to arrange the blocks into two rows of two blocks each. Sew the blocks in each row together. Press the seam allowances open. Sew the rows together. Press the seam allowances open.

Quilt finished size: 44½" x 44½"

Blocks and finished sizes:

Twin Star: 12" x 12"

Square in a Square: 4" x 4"

2. Refer to "Borders with Butted Corner" (page 15) to sew the black 1½"-wide first-border strips to the quilt top, adding the top and bottom borders first, and then the sides. Press the seam allowances toward the border.

3. Using the patterns (page 95) and referring to "Paper Foundation Piecing" (page 7), trace eight *each* of border patterns A and B onto your paper-piecing foundation material. Paper piece the border strips in numerical order using the bright print 2" x 3" rectangles.

4. Join two paper-pieced A strips and two paper-pieced B strips end to end to make a second-border strip. Repeat to make a total of four strips. Sew pieced strips to the top and bottom edges of the quilt top. Press the seam allowances toward the first border. Join black or gray 2½" squares to both ends of the remaining two pieced borders. Press the seam allowances toward the squares. Add these strips to the sides of the quilt top. Press the seam allowances toward the first border.

5. Repeat step 2 to add the black 1½"-wide third-border strips to the quilt top. Press the seam allowances toward the third border.

6. Refer to "Paper Foundation Piecing" (page 7) to trace 36 copies of the Square-in-a-Square block pattern (page 95) onto your paper-piecing foundation material. Paper piece the blocks in numerical order using the black or dark gray 4" squares for piece 1 and four matching bright-print triangles for the remaining pieces.

7. Sew eight Square-in-a-Square blocks together side by side to make a top border strip. Repeat to make a total of two border strips. Sew these borders to the top and bottom edges of the quilt top. Press the seam allowance toward the third border. Join 10 blocks together in the same manner for the side border. Repeat to make a total of two borders. Sew these borders to the sides of the quilt top. Press the seam allowances toward the third border.

8. Repeat step 2 to add the black 2½"-wide fifth-border strips to the quilt top. Press the seam allowances toward the fifth border.

Finishing the Quilt

Refer to "Happy Endings" (page 17) as needed.

1. Layer the quilt top with batting and backing; baste.

2. Quilt as desired.

3. Square up the quilt top.

4. Add a rod pocket if desired and bind the quilt with the black 2"-wide strips.

5. Stitch a label to the quilt back.

Quilt assembly

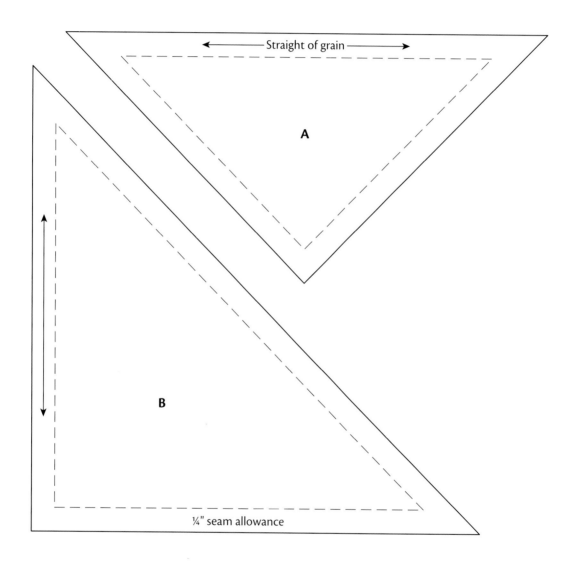

Straight of grain

A

B

¼" seam allowance

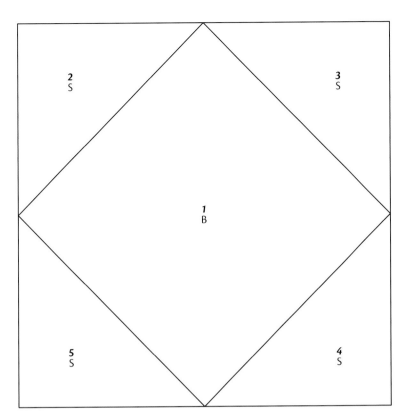

Fabric Key

B—Black/dark gray print
S—Bright scrap

**Square-in-a-Square Block
Foundation Pattern**

**Border A
Foundation Pattern**

**Border B
Foundation Pattern**

Resource

½" precut hexagon templates
Paper Pieces
P.O. Box 68
Sycamore, IL 60178
(800) 337-1537
FAX: (815) 899-2900
www.paperpieces.com

About the Author

This is Jaynette's fifth book with Martingale & Company, but her first about making scrappy quilts. Jaynette's interest in scrap quilts came about as a result of her continued love of quilting and her growing fabric stash. It was also inspired by other quilters' responses to seeing scrap quilts during her quilt guild's show-and-tell segments. Quilters would always "oooh" and "aaah."

Not normally a scrap-quilt lover or maker, Jaynette began to study scrap quilts in books and on display, trying to understand their appeal. It was only upon completion of a guild quilt challenge to use *ugly* fabric pieces given to her in a brown paper sack that she recognized the answer: you can't do just one or two blocks. A scrap quilt's beauty comes from many, many blocks. When you arrange many, many scrappy blocks, their differences in colors and prints become like cracked glass: they sparkle in the sunlight, they catch your attention when you least expect it, and they make you feel "warm and cozy." Her scrap-quilt journey had begun.

Jaynette has also learned one other scrap-quilt truth: Just because you use your scrap strips and bits and make lots of scrappy quilts, your fabric stash does not become smaller! You must persevere!

Jaynette lives in Conway, Arkansas, with her husband, Larry, and their cat and dog, Inky and Buddy.